Auld Enemies

Auld Enemies

The Scots and the English

David Ross

**Illustrated by
James Hutcheson**

Birlinn

First published in 2002 by
Birlinn Limited
West Newington House
10 Newington Road
Edinburgh
EH9 1QS

www.birlinn.co.uk

ISBN 1 84158 243 3

British Library Cataloguing-in-Publication Data
A catalogue record for this book is available
from the British Library

Typeset by Textype, Cambridge
Printed and bound by Cox & Wyman Ltd, Reading

For my Scoto-English children

Scotland is not wholly surrounded by the sea –
unfortunately.
Hugh MacDiarmid, The Sea, *in* Scottish Scene

It is very rare to find a foreigner, other than an American,
who can distinguish between English and Scots.
George Orwell, The Lion and the Unicorn

The well-bred Englishman is about as agreeable a fellow as
you can find anywhere – especially, as I have noted, if he
is an Irishman or a Scotchman.
Finley Peter Dunne, Mr Dooley Remembers

The fact is, there is no such thing as national character.
There are, however, plenty of stupid prejudices
masquerading as scholarly enquiry into how and why we
are different from the English.
James Murphy, in The Herald, *1992*

The Englishman and the Scot have long served as one
another's *alter ego*.
Karl Miller, Doubles

What ethic river is this wondrous Tweed
Whose one bank vertue, other vice doth breed?
Andrew Marvell, The Loyal Scot

CONTENTS

INTRODUCTION

In the year 2002, invoking an article of Common Law dating from the Middle Ages, a judge in Plymouth, England, formally debarred a Scottish defendant from entering upon English soil for a period of five years. The case aroused considerable interest, not least because Scotland and England have been politically united as a single nation state, with no internal border, for nearly three hundred years. Internal exile seemed more like a judgment from imperial Russia than democratic Great Britain. The nature of the offence – disorderly behaviour and breach of the peace, with alcohol playing a significant part – and the unusual sentence, provided a reminder that ancient attitudes and stereotypes are by no means forgotten. Great Britain continues to harbour three nations, England, Scotland and Wales, each with a strong sense of identity and its own range of jealously guarded traditions. With countries as with householders, the nearest neighbours are always the best-known, though not invariably the best-loved. The very closeness of the perspective can distort small oddities and dissimilarities into large differences. The Scots and the English can still get up one other's noses.

Scotland became a unified kingdom in 1034. England's identity stems from the Norman Conquest of 1066. At certain times before that, it had seemed possible that the Scottish realm would extend as far as the Humber, taking in all of Northumbria and Cumbria. Such a division of the island – Wales apart – would have created two states of comparable size, and led to a history that might have been very different. As it was, the fixing of a frontier from the Solway across the Cheviot Hills to the Tweed confirmed an unequal relationship. Scotland was going to have to live with the fact that England was much bigger, more populous, and richer. England was also in the way. Sea-lanes to north, east and south-west were open to the Scots, but the land-route south towards the rest of Europe was blocked. The resulting rivalry was well-known on the continent, even rating a line in Dante's *Divine Comedy*. In *Paradiso* the poet comments: 'There shall be seen that pride that quickens thirst, that makes the Scot and the Englishman mad, so that neither can keep within his own bounds.'

For seven hundred years, successive English kings and governments would make use of their geographical position and their wealth to keep the northern kingdom isolated. As a result, Scotland was poorer than it might have been, but also more dangerous and violent as a neighbour. For five hundred years, the English maintained the hope of absorbing Scotland into their own realm, or at least of reducing it to a form of tributary status, in which it could do no harm. While Scotland could not reasonably hope to overrun and conquer England, it certainly had the power to inflict heavy damage. Furthermore, from an early stage in national history, the Scots made a bond with England's other neighbours, the French. In official and unofficial concert with the Gaels of Ireland, the Scots also helped to delay the full English conquest of that country for centuries. Never once until 1603 did the Scots form any sort of military alliance with the English. Indeed, when the young King James I, an involuntary guest of the English Henry V, was taken on campaign in France, he found himself facing the army of his own countrymen. It had been sent to help the French by the government of Scotland, acting in his name. To England, the continuing independence of Scotland was a threat and a distraction.

Even in 1603, when James Stewart, great-great-grandson of Henry VII of England (and of fifteen other persons including French, Burgundians and Scots), achieved his long-awaited status as James I of England as well as James VI of Scotland, his native country remained a poor relation. Ironically, having got the Scots' king, the English no longer wanted the Scots' territory. The sting had been drawn from the north, they believed, and they thought that Scotland would be a drain on England's wealth. For their own part, the Scots went to war to resist the attempts of the Stewart kings to standardise religion in the two kingdoms. Political union between the two countries was finally brought about, in controversial circumstances, in 1707. This did not mark the end of hostilities, either. Slightly less than forty years later, an army of Highlanders invaded England and got to within 120 miles of London.

The battle of Culloden in 1746, fought not between Scots and English, but between Jacobites and Hanoverians (with many Scots among the latter), marks the end of large-scale armed conflict as a means of resolving political differences within the island of Great Britain. Since then, the inhabitants have increasingly followed a 'British' way of life, in their own Scottish, Welsh or English manner. But because Britishness is still an outer layer of identity, felt in the mind rather than in the heart, the old attitudes and rivalries, formed in a very different context, remain, although they are normally expressed in a very much tamer and more playful form nowadays. The last time there was a strong sense of British identity was during the Second World War, but even then more local attitudes often prevailed. The story is told of a fishing boat from north-east Scotland, which happened to be at the English port of Lowestoft in June 1940, when the call went out for all available vessels to help in bringing the retreating British army back across the Channel from Dunkirk. The skipper took his boat through shot and shell, as close inshore as he could get, and surveying the milling

troops on the shore and in the water, bellowed: 'Onybody here fae Peterheid or the Broch?'

To newer arrivals in the British population, and to the outside world, these attitudes may seem eccentric or bizarre, perhaps even unhealthy. Taking a more positive view, they may show that Britain's mingled culture finds a way of coming to terms with a long history containing its full share of bitterness and bloodshed.

It is in that positive spirit that this book is written. To an extent, it shows the English not as the Scots really see them, but as the Scots feel they should be shown, in case they should become too big for their already very large boots. Equally, it shows the Scots not as the English really see them, but as the English feel they should be shown, because otherwise the Scots might become so big-headed as to be totally intolerable.

Mutual comparisons between Scots and English have been distorted by the presence in the same group of islands of another large national group – the Irish. The Irish have been better than the Scots at keeping a national identity over the last three hundred or so years. They have placed themselves, by choice as well as geography, off-side. The Scots, who in the Middle Ages had much more in common with the Irish than they did with the English, later found themselves sharing ever more characteristics with the Sassenachs. In the tripartite relationship, the Irish ended up as the butts – but they can defend themselves well. In a three-cornered relationship story between a Scotsman, an Englishman, and a native of any other country, it is almost invariably the third who will come off worst. The only exception is when a particular weakness is being explored, like the Scottish sense of economy:

A Scotsman, an Englishman and a Welshman went into a pub together, and each ordered a pint of black stout. It was a hot day, and as luck would have it, a fly settled into the froth on top of each pint. The Englishman made a face and pushed his glass away. The Welshman put his finger into the froth, scooped out the fly, and blew it away, before having a drink. The Scotsman reached in very carefully with two fingers, lifting the fly out by a leg. He held it up above the glass.

'Come on, ye wee devil,' he commanded, 'spit it oot.'

The mass of English people did not know the Scots very well until the mid-eighteenth century. They knew the Welsh better, and there are more jokes and rude stories in old English chap-books about Taffy than there are about Sawney. They knew the Irish better too, and once again Irish jokes precede and greatly outnumber jokes about Scots in the early eighteenth century. But by the end of that century a stereotyped English view of the Scots was firmly in place. The Scots did not have a similar caricature of the English. This was partly because the English displayed such variety, from canny, blunt-spoken northerners to their phlegmatic southern country-folk and effervescent Cockneys. As the Scottish writer Christopher Harvie remarks: ' "Englishness" ' has always been notoriously hard to define – definitions, anyhow, are not the sort of thing chaps go in for' (from *Travelling Scot*). But there was another reason. The English created a Scottish type, an individual personality, however much of a distortion it was. The Scots saw the English not in individual terms but as a mass, a vast group, made up of disparate elements and united in only one thing – they were the other side, the opposition, the 'Auld Enemy'.

THE ANGLO-SCOTS

The 'auld enemy' view of the English explains why Scots who went too far in assimilating themselves to an English style were regarded as renegades. The 'Anglo-Scots' were seen as Scottish folk for whom Scotland – and so all other Scots – was not good enough. There were few extenuating circumstances.

. . . we do not rate highly the Scotsman who has succeeded in becoming an Englishman, unless his Rugby is exceptionally good.
James Bridie (1888–1951), One Way of Living

Torquils, Jamies and Fionas turn tartan at the right season, roughly coinciding with the annual northward migration of the royals.
Christopher Harvie, Travelling Scot *(1999)*

*

The most outspoken critic of the Anglo-Scot was the poet Hugh MacDiarmid, who in one fine raking sweep condemned: '. . . the whole gang of high mucky-mucks, famous fatheads, old wives of both sexes, stuffed shirts, hollow men with headpieces stuffed with straw, bird-wits, lookers-under-beds, trained seals, creeping Jesuses, Scots Wha Ha'evers, village idiots, policemen, leaders of white-mouse factions and noted connoisseurs of bread and butter . . . and all the touts and toadies and lickspittles of the English Ascendancy, and their infernal womenfolk, and all their skunkoil skulduggery.' (*Lucky Poet*)

*

It is significant that there is no generic name for those few English people whose aspirations went the other way, and who tried to be as Scottish as the Scots, if not more so. In some parts of Scotland 'white settler' is used, though it is meant for those who do not conform to local *mores*. But some of their English fellow-countrymen might say there is a phrase to cover the situation – 'going native'.

AN AWFUL TRUTH

Over the years, the Scots have given much thought to the English – much more than the English have given to the Scots. In fact, it is one of the Scots' beefs against the English that, most of the time, they don't seem to even notice Scotland is there. In the mid-nineteenth century, the Scottish academic J. S. Blackie was talking to Dr Benjamin Jowett, of Oxford University.

'I hope you in Oxford don't think we hate you?'

'We don't think about you,' was the reply.

Three hundred years before that, Lord Clarendon had noted that 'when the whole nation was solicitous to know what passed weekly in Germany and Poland and all other parts of Europe, no man ever enquired what was doing in Scotland, nor had that kingdom a place or mention in one page of any gazette, so little the world heard or thought of that people'.

The same thought was echoed by the Scottish writer Alastair Reid, in a *New Yorker* survey of the Scots, from 1964: 'Of all the grievances nursed by the Scots, none is greater than the fact that the English apparently do not bother to hate back.'

The reason is that they have no reason to do so: apart from the much-invaded inhabitants of northern England, for whom 'Scotch' was a dirty word during the Middle Ages, the English had very little knowledge of the country, or reason to acquire any. Even in the mid-twentieth century, Trevor Royle, as an English child living in Scotland, noted that his English relatives viewed Scotland as a complete popular stereotype: 'a country of quaint, hairy-kneed and parsimonious old men who went about muttering into their whisky: "It's a braw bricht moonlicht nicht the nicht, ye ken."'

Paradoxically, however, the English have written much more about Scotland and the Scots than the Scots have about England. From the sixteenth century until the twentieth, a succession of English travellers wrote about their impressions of the country to the north, and of its people. One or two were filled with hostile prejudice, but most tried to be fair. There are no equivalents from Scotland; those Scots who wrote about life in England had no interest in explaining the idiosyncrasies of the country to their fellow Scots. The reason for this imbalance is that for the English, Scotland was an exotic place, rich in the differences and discomforts essential to give zest and interest to a travelogue. For the Scots, England did not offer the same opportunities. The amenities of England were too well known to bear description. Its attractions were not found in wild country, uncouth habits, homes and language, but in superior comforts, laden tables, good roads, and urbane gatherings at places like Bath. Incoming Scots, mostly from the wealthier or aspiring sections of society, took these things almost instantly for granted, and would never have shown themselves so unsophisticated as to write books about them.

SOME ASPECTS OF ENGLISHNESS

1. The Bumptious Englishman

The John Bull-ish heartiness of a certain type of Englishman is something that irks many Scots. They do not see it as genuine openness but as ostentation, or even as a cover for a more sinister attitude. The Englishman's jovial smile is merely a trick to lull you into a false sense of security before he runs off with your property. A modern Gaelic poem sums up this suspicious point of view:

Cheers!
The lads arrived one day
In the pub
Nattering in Gaelic.

And a big posh Englishman arrived amongst them,
Full of surprise at their chat,
And offered them a dram,
And they accepted it with alacrity,
And then another,
And another and another.

And, in parting,
He asked them, perhaps,
To drink his own health
In their own language,
And they raised their glasses
And cried out in Gaelic as one:
Good health, you arsehole!
(From Gaelic)

An older and more subtle example of the same thing comes from a resort village in Galloway. A jolly English gent and his family had been coming to the place for several summers, and felt they knew it and its inhabitants well. As the Englishman was strolling down the village street one day, he passed one of the residents, standing by his front door. Close by there was a fat pig, rootling about in the gutter.

'Morning, Sandy,' called the visitor, then, nodding at the pig: 'Is that a friend of yours?'

'No, no,' said the native, quietly. 'Just an acquaintance, same as yourself.'

An even earlier example comes from the seventeenth century, by which time Scots who had business with the king came regularly to London. One of these was a tall, burly Highlander, Sir Robert Bleakie, of Blair Atholl. While in London, he was invited to a dinner party where there was a mixed gathering of English and Scots. After the bottle had passed round a few times, and the spirits of the assembly began to rise, an English general, a trooper of fame and a noted *bon viveur*, rose to speak.

'Gentlemen, when I am in my cups, and the wine begins to warm my blood, I have an absurd custom of railing against the Scots. Knowing my weakness, I hope no member of the company will take it amiss.'

Bleakie in turn rose up, and replied, with perfect simplicity and good nature.

'Gentlemen, I too must confess to a weakness. When I am in my cups, and the wine warms my blood, if I hear a man rail against the Scotch, I have an absurd custom of immediately kicking him out of the room. Knowing my weakness, I hope no gentleman will take it amiss.'

On that occasion, it was noted that the general did not follow his usual custom.

2. The English Intellectual

What is it about the English and intellectuals? ... an English intellectual is either not English or else, if his papers are invincibly in order, not an intellectual ... The English behave as if intellectuals were unicorns: if you see one, you know it isn't one.

Neal Ascherson, Games with Shadows *(1988)*

*

In their exchange of letters about the English, published as *A Small Stir*, James Bridie and Moray McLaren enjoyed having a go at that 'most secluded thing, an English intellectual,' and the 'thin, high note of sneering denigration which sounds through so much of their able, sometimes brilliant writing'. Highbrow English writers, said Bridie, 'write admirably... It looks like nonsense. It smells like nonsense. It tastes like nonsense. I believe it is nonsense. But perhaps that is also a characteristic of the English, that they write nonsense really well.'

*

The intellectual qualities of English and anglicising writers were also assailed by Hugh MacDiarmid in *Gairmscoile*:

Ablachs, and scrats, and dorbels o' a' kinds
Aye'd drob me wi' their puir ell-dronin' minds,
Wee drochlin' craturs drutling their bit thochts
The dorty bodies! Feech! Nae Sassunach drings
'll daunton me.

It was MacDiarmid who described London literary critics as recalling to him 'that extraordinary chirruping conversation which sounds almost human but, on investigation with an electric torch, is found to be merely a couple of hedgehogs courting beneath one's window.' (*Lucky Poet*)

*

3. The Cool Englishman

Among the English characteristics recognised and appreciated by the Scots is a coolness or *sang-froid* – an opposite characteristic to their own supposed *perfervidum ingenium*, or fervency of mind.

A group of English football supporters were drinking quietly in a Glasgow bar, when in came a huge red-haired man wearing a Scotland shirt and a kilt, and with his face painted in a blue and white saltire.

'All English skunks get oota here!' he bellowed, and advanced threateningly.

The visitors took one look at him and fled, without waiting to finish their drinks. All except one, who continued to stand calmly at the bar.

'My, there certainly were a lot of them, weren't there!' he said.

*

A Scot was paying a weekend visit to an English business acquaintance's home. On the first evening, quite by accident, he entered the wrong bathroom and found his host's wife in the bath. Hurriedly retreating, he sought out his host, who was downstairs, and apologetically explained his misadventure.

The Englishman looked up from his newspaper.
'Skinny old thing, isn't she?' he remarked.

*

4. The Formal Englishman

The English stiff upper lip is something Scots like to poke
fun at. A once popular comic story told of the three
Englishmen, survivors of a shipwreck, who were washed up
on a desert island. For five years they never exchanged a
word, as they had not been introduced to one other. The
Scots like to think that they are less hidebound by formality
than the English.

*

A Glaswegian, used to sharing taxis with strangers, was
queuing for a taxi at Euston Station, when he heard a man
give the driver an address in the same street that he wanted.
Quickly moving to the head of the line, he jumped into the
same cab. Clasping his suitcase on his knees, he turned to
the other passenger and said, pleasantly:
    'My name's Buchanan.'
    'Mine', said the other, chillily, 'is not.'

*

5. The Mean-Spirited Englishman

There are relatively few Scottish stories about mean
Englishmen. Meanness is not seen as a typical English
characteristic, and aggressive humour, with its instinct to go
for the exposed jugular, finds other targets. But an English
refusal to accept, and respect, Scottish customs is bound to
attract criticism.

A wealthy English tenant had taken over a Scottish laird's

shooting lodge for the season. Included among the fixtures and fittings was the resident piper, MacKillop. His function was to play the bagpipes outside at breakfast-time, and to come into the dining-room after dinner to play a *pibroch*. Between these times he did nothing, and the tenant resented this. He also resented that each evening the butler placed a tumbler full of malt whisky on the table for MacKillop to consume before he began to play. He calculated that the piper was getting through a bottle of the expensive stuff in a week. One evening he ordered the butler to leave out a glass of water instead of whisky. The water was ignored, and the playing that night was terrible. Even the tenant noticed, and a Scottish neighbour, who was a guest, beckoned to the piper as he paused between tunes and said:

'Something wrong with the pipes tonight, MacKillop?'

'Aye,' said MacKillop. 'Dry. They need whisky, malt whisky.'

His eye was fixed meaningfully on the tenant, who, not wishing to seem mean in front of his guests, asked the butler to provide a glass of whisky. MacKillop downed it in one.

'I thought you said it was for the pipes!' cried the tenant, stung to protest.

'Aye, but it needs blawing into them,' said MacKillop.

*

6. The Riotous English

... rioting is a recurrent English activity with a long history ... Rioting is at least as English as thatched cottages and honey still for tea ... Rioting ... is the traditional resort of those who feel excluded and oppressed by the social and political structure under which – rather than in which – they live.

Neal Ascherson, Games with Shadows *(1988)*

*

7. The Ruthless Englishman

Whenever I hear of English ruthlessness in some remote place, I always imagine it being expressed (if it can be expressed in words at all) in a homely North of England accent. 'You boogers 'ave asked for it, and by goom, you're going to get it.' Then, with smiling countenance, the Englishman proceeds to lam into his opponent and destroy him, rules or no rules.

Moray McLaren, A Small Stir

THE CANNY SCOT

'Canny', the adjective most frequently linked with 'Scot', is a most interesting word, with a whole range of meanings packed into it. No single term corresponds exactly, but among the most common are cautious, prudent, shrewd. One of the numerous Scots words borrowed into standard English, it is used by the English to describe the Scots when they don't want to be rude to them. 'Canny Scot' as a description combines relief at getting the right word – the English like to know whom they're dealing with – and a certain friendly but wary respect for the qualities it implies.

Three men came along to pay their respects after the death of a friend. They were an Irishman, and Englishman, and a Scotsman. As they looked on their former acquaintance in his coffin, the Irishman said:

'He was always generous. He once lent me ten pounds and I never paid it back. Now I will.'

And he took a ten-pound note from his wallet and put it in the coffin.

'He lent me money too,' said the Englishman. 'Twenty pounds – and he never asked for it back.'

He produced a twenty-pound note and placed it in the coffin.

'And me,' sighed the Scot. 'He lent me fifty pounds, and I never got round to paying it back. But now it's time.'

Bringing out cheque-book and pen, he wrote out a cheque for eighty pounds. Placing it reverently in the coffin, he removed the two bank-notes and put them in his pocket.

*

Scots can however be too canny for their own good:

'I never get a decent cup of coffee,' sighed Sandy.

'Why is that?'

'Well, when I'm at home, I don't like to put more than one teaspoonful of sugar in, because of the cost. When I'm given coffee by someone else, I always ask for three teaspoonfuls, to make the most of the chance. But I really only like coffee with two sugars.'

*

A young Scot was questioned by his friend:
    'Is it true that you've fallen for that bonny Jeannie McAllister?'
    'Well, I very nearly did,' was the answer. 'I was going to take her to the pictures.'
    'What went wrong?'
'She wouldna go Dutch on the tickets.'

*

Being a financially prudent man, Mr MacPherson was rather upset when he accidentally let a 50p piece fall into the public toilet. What shall I do? he wondered. Is it worth delving in there for 50p? Then he had a brainwave. Reaching into his pocket, he found another 50p piece, and dropped it in too. A pound's another matter entirely, he thought, rolling up his sleeve.

*

The famous capacity of the Scots for being rational can be exaggerated into the humour of 'irrational rationality'. An

Aberdonian was walking along the road when he came upon a discarded crutch. He picked it up, took it home, and broke his wife's leg.

*

As a footnote to canniness, here is a Scots view (by Robert Ford) of the English view of the Scot:

Land o' canny, careful bodies –
Foes to a' ungodly fun;
Those who sum up man's whole duty –
Heaven, Hell and Number One.

THE CLEVER SCOT . . . AND THE STUPID ENGLISHMAN

In the long war of words and wit that has characterised the Scots' relations with the English at least since the thirteenth century, the Scots have been identified at various times as mean, dour, greedy, boastful, gauche, flea-bitten, poverty-stricken, unwashed, drunken and a number of other things. But whatever insults are slung north over the Border, no-one has ever seriously denied one crucial thing about the Scots – they are smarter. The English can poke fun at the Scots in many ways, but a joke that shows an Englishman outsmarting a Scot would be most unusual. Scottish humour makes the most of this.

'How's your brother Donald?'
'Oh, he's never been the same since his accident. They had to remove a third of his brain, you know.'
'Oh dear, where is he, then?'
'We sent him to England. He's doing fine there.'
'Which hospital?'
'Who said anything about a hospital?'

*

A Scotsman once asked an Englishman if he'd heard the joke about the skull of William Shakespeare, aged twelve, being put on display at Stratford on Avon. 'No,' said the Englishman, 'what is it?'

*

Scottish jokes about English stupidity are centred on a basic supposition that the English are just not very bright. They don't get the point quickly enough. But sometimes the Englishman's stupidity can rebound on the smart Scots:

Two Scotsmen and an Englishmen were imprisoned in a Middle Eastern jail. After a long time, they unearthed a dirty old lamp in the corner. It proved to be an Aladdin-type lamp complete with genie, who duly offered each of them a wish.

'I wish I was home in Edinburgh,' said the first Scotsman. And he vanished.

'I wish I was home in Glasgow,' said the second, and he too disappeared.

The Englishman scratched his head.

'I don't know if I want to be in London with my mum or in Manchester with my girl-friend,' he said. 'I wish my pals were here to help me decide.'

And, in a flash, they were.

*

How do you get an Englishman's brain to the size of a pea?
  Inflate it.

*

What do you call an Englishman with an IQ of 75?
  The Managing Director.

*

Guide in the Royal Scottish Museum: 'These Egyptian carvings are more than three thousand years old. Perhaps Moses saw them, when he was a boy.'

English visitor: 'I never knew Moses had been to Edinburgh.'

*

Two cars collided somewhere in the Borders. One was driven by an Englishman, the other by a Scot. They were uninjured, but the damage made it impossible for either to drive away. As they waited for the police to arrive, the Scot produced a bottle of whisky and hospitably offered it first to the Englishman.

'Calms the nerves, after a shake-up like that,' he said.

But when the Englishman handed back the bottle after taking a hefty swig, the Scot put it away without drinking any.

'Aren't you having some too?' asked the Englishman.

'I'll wait until the police have been,' was the answer.

*

An Englishman's wife finally got him a job as a doorman in a big office block. At the end of the first day she asked him how he got on.

'It was all right with the doors marked PUSH and PULL,' he said. 'I finally got those worked out. But I had terrible trouble all day with the one marked LIFT.'

The novelist Tobias Smollett, in the mid-eighteenth century, expressed the intellectual Scotsman's view of the southern neighbours: 'I am heartily tired of this Land of Indifference and Phlegm where the finer Sensations of the Soul are not felt, and Felicity is held to consist in stupefying Port and overgrown Buttocks of Beef, where Genius is lost, and Taste altogether extinguished.' (Not that Smollett was seriously tempted to return to the dubious refinements of his native land).

*

Even more Scottish jokes deal with the outsmarting of English visitors who come to Scotland ('stung by everything and everyone' in the words of the writer John R. Allan). Most of these take the form of the put-down. However, the fact that Americans receive similar treatment may suggest that it is rich, self-satisfied visitors who are satirised in such jokes rather than the English in particular. In these cases, of course, the visitor is always set up in advance, made to be boastful or pompous or both:

An American visitor hired a Glasgow cabby to take him on a tour of some of the sights. He wasn't very impressed by the Clyde:

'We've got wider ditches than that where I live,' he drawled. When they came in sight of Ben Lomond, he remarked:

'Does that pass for a mountain round here? Where I come from, they'd say that was a hillock.'

Of Loch Lomond, he said: 'I know gardens in the USA that pond could be fitted into.'

'It could be arranged,' said the cabby.

'How do you mean?' asked the American.

'All ye need is a wee pipe to lay across the Atlantic, and if ye can sook as weel as ye can blaw, ye'll hae the whole o't ower in nae time.'

*

It would be easy to dismiss all such jokes as small-country humour, as with New Zealand *vs* Australia, or Canada (or anyone) *vs* the USA, and therefore expressing a real sense of inferiority under the guise of seeming superior. But would it be true of Scotland? Under its exterior cloak of reserve, the country of 'Here's tae us – wha's like us?' has got a good conceit of itself. This is potentially a dangerous weakness, of course. Complacency comes before a tumble (as the Scottish soccer side has experienced on more than one occasion). The eighteenth-century English writer Anthony Powell noted it in his diatribe *Caledonia*:

> Such Mediocrity was ne'er on view,
> Bolster'd by tireless Scottish Ballyhoo –
> Nay! In two qualities they stand supreme:
> Their self-advertisement and their self-esteem.

At least one joke brands both sides as equally dumb:

Scotsman: Guess how many ferrets I've got in this bag, and I'll give you both of them.

Englishman: Five?

Scotsman: That's near enough.

INTERCHANGEABLE JOKES

If an English–Scottish joke can be reversed simply by switching the names round, it's not the genuine article, but one of those all-too-common international jokes that flit around from place to place, impersonal and ineffective. The humorous equivalent of a raspberry, it hardly expresses any feeling and fails to prick the skin.

Tell me one thing that's wrong with England/Scotland?
   It's above sea-level.

How do you stop an Englishman/Scotsman jumping into the River Thames/Clyde?
   You don't.

Have you heard the latest about the English/Scottish car-workers?
   They've abolished clocking on in the factory. Now, when they drop in, they just sign the visitors' book.

You can always tell a Scotsman/Englishman – but you can't tell him much.

ANGLO-SAXON ATTITUDES

'True blue' is originally a dyer's term, indicating a kind of blue which does not fade, and from that its sense has been extended to the steadfast, unswerving nature of the idealised

English person.

'I was born a true Englishman, all my life I've been a true Englishman, and I hope to die a true Englishman,' proclaimed the – needless to say – Englishman.

'Man, have ye nae ambeetion?' inquired his Scottish friend.

*

The clubbish, coded world of England has always been a mystery to Scots, and even those who successfully joined it, like John Buchan, never felt quite at home. One who felt its combination of insidious charm and alienness was Ralph Glasser, in his memoir *Gorbals Boy at Oxford*. He is speaking of his friends James and Bill, 'grown-up school prefects, descendants of Stalky & Co . . . they would always be the fixers, the cool-headed operators, the secretive network of power that I would never be permitted to join'. Bill summed it up for his benefit. 'You're too fundamental for the likes of us. We are just the operators behind the scenes! We enjoy the game, that's all. We have no principles, really, except to keep the *status quo* – the game as we know it.'

*

'Scotland costs us, nags us, and grinds on. She may be surprised at how easily and comfortably we let her go.'

Edward Pearce, The Guardian, *January 1992*

The English have never bothered to define their national identity. Instead there are phrases: the tautologous 'we know who we are,' or the comfortable 'we govern ourselves pretty decently.'

Neal Ascherson, Games with Shadows

*

'If I had a wish,' sighed the Englishman, 'it would be to build a twenty-foot high wall round the whole of England, to protect it from every kind of foreign influence.'

'If I had a wish,' said the Scotsman, 'it would be to fill the whole thing with water to the brim.'

CALEDONIAN ATTITUDES

Back in the fifteenth century, 'Englishman' was a term of insult in Scotland. In one of the contests of poetic vituperation known as flytings, Walter Kennedy observes of William Dunbar (who came from Lothian):

> In Ingland, owle, suld by thuyne habitacione,
> Homage to Edward Langshankis maid thy kyn.

(You owl, you should be living in England; your forebears paid homage to Edward Longshanks.)

*

I am sure my bones would not rest in an English grave, or my clay mix with the earth of that country. I believe the thought would drive me mad on my death-bed could I suppose that any of my friends would be base enough to convey my carcase back to her soil. I would not even feed her worms if I could help it.

Lord Byron (but he was not considering Scotland as the alternative)

*

English visitors to Scotland are liable to gentle or ungentle teasing, but it was not always so. Thomas Pennant in the eighteenth century commented on the good manners of the Highlanders: 'Thro' my whole tour I never met with a single instance of national [i.e. anti-English] reflection!

Their forbearance proves them to be superior to the meanness of retaliation; I fear they pity us, but I hope not indiscriminately.' Pennant's visit was in 1769; the duke of Cumberland's oppressive treatment of the Highlanders after Culloden was twenty years in the past but by no means forgotten.

*

The famous Socialist agitator, John Maclean, on trial in 1916, admitted to using the words 'bloody English capitalists', but he pleaded that it was simply a classical expression.

VERSIONS OF HISTORY

One of the oldest jibes cast at the English by the Scots was that England, unlike Scotland, had been a conquered nation. And that not once, but *four* times – by Romans, Saxons, Danes and Normans:

> For our Heretage was ever Free,
> Since *Scota* of *Aegypt* tuik the Sea,
> Whilst ye have ever Conquered been:
> For a Thousand Pounds of Gold schein
> To *Julius Caesar* payit yee
> Of tribute, thus ye was not free;
> With *Saxons* syne ye were orthrawn . . .

In this anonymous poem, the four conquests of England are listed, culminating with:

> A Bastard came out of Normandy,
> Conquest Ingland all hailily.   [entirely]

This war of words was still going strong some three hundred years later, when a Scottish writer, G. Steel, in

1700, during the period of hostility before the Union, invented a dialogue between kings Robert III of Scotland and Henry IV of England, in which the former says:

> Thus four times thirled and overhald,
>   [bound and conquered]
> You're the great refuse of all the warld.

*

In the fifteenth century, another anonymous Scot assailed the English pretension, stemming from Geoffrey of Monmouth (and with the serious aim of asserting England's primacy within Britain), that Brutus, 'noblest Roman of them all', was its founding father. The Scots preferred to parade their own equally improbable origin from Scota, daughter of Pharaoh. At the same time the writer throws a barb at Pope Gregory the Great's famous reported comment, noted in Bede's *History of the English Church* and cherished by later Anglo-Saxon generations, that Anglian slaves in the Roman market were 'Not Angles, but Angels':

> Ye, Inglische hursone, sumtyme will avant
>   [whoreson, boast]
> Your progeny from Brutus to haif tane,   [taken]
> And sumtyme from ane angell or ane sanct,
> As Angelus and Anglus both war ane.

> Angellis in erth yit hard I few or nane,   [heard]
> Except the feyndis with Lucifer that fell.
> Avant you, villane, of that lord allane,
> Tak thy progeny from Pluto, prince of Hell.

> Because ye use in hoillis to hyd your sell, [holes]
> Anglus is cum from Angulus in deid.
> Above all uderis Brutus bure the bell
> Quha slew his fader, houping to succeid.

> Than chus you ane of thais, I rek not ader: [care]
> Tak Beelzebub or Brutus to be your fader.

If it was angels, says the poet, it must have been from the fallen angels that the English were descended. Anyway, Angle comes from *angulus* (a dark corner). And furthermore Brutus killed his own father to speed up his inheritance. Take your pick, I don't mind. According to your own claim, you are either descended from the Devil or from Brutus the parricide.

*

It was an ancient conceit of the Scots – borrowed from the French according to an eminent scholar – to pretend that the English were born with tails. The legend goes back to a story that an Englishman pinned a tail upon St Augustine, and so his nation was appropriately punished by God, who inflicted tails upon them. In one of the legends of William Wallace, his famous confrontation with the English soldiers in Lanark (1296) began when he protected a small boy who had put his fingers behind his back and waggled them like a tail at the angry pikemen.

In one of the flytings, or abuse contests, of Scottish poets in the reign of James IV we find these lines:

> Thy forefader maid irisch & irisch men thin
> Throu his tresoun broght inglis rumplis in.
>
> [English tails]

*

A curious reference is made in the anonymous *Voyage of Kynge Edwarde*, describing the English king's invasion of Scotland in 1298, to the abbot of Aberbrothock (Arbroath), who 'made the people of Scotlande beleve theat there was but women and no men in Englande'. Whether the abbot believed that the English nation was half composed of cross-dressing females, or whether he was merely ascribing a certain femininity to Englishmen, akin to the 'mincing Jeremies' gibes of a later time, remains unclear.

*

Complacent in their possession of an apostle as patron saint, the Scots also dwelt on the dubious origin of England's chosen saint:

> To save a maid St George a dragon slew,
> A brave exployt if all that's said is true,
> Some think there are no dragons; nay, 'tis said
> There was no George; pray God there was a maid.

Anonymous lines on England's patron saint, eighteenth century, from J. Maidment, Book of Scottish Pasquils *(1866)*

GENERALITIES FROM BOTH SIDES OF THE BORDER

Lang beards heartless, painted hoods witless, gay coats graceless, mak' England thriftless.

Early Scottish view of the English

*

A fiery ettercap,   [spider]
A fractious chiel,
As het as ginger,   [hot]
And as stieve as steel.

Characterisation of the medieval Scot

*

For every nation regards another nation as barbarous when
their two natures and complexions are contrary to theirs,
and there are not two nations under the firmament that are
more contrary and different to each other than Englishmen
and Scotsmen, howbeit they be within one island, and of
one language. For Englishmen are subtle and Scotsmen
facile, Englishmen are ambitious in prosperity and
Scotsmen are humane in prosperity, Englishmen are
humble when they are subdued by force and violence, and
Scotsmen are furious when they are violently subdued.
Englishmen are cruel when they get victory, and Scotsmen
are merciful when they get victory. And to conclude, it is
impossible that Scotsmen and Englishmen can remain in
concord under one government because their natures and
conditions are as different as is the nature of sheep and
wolves.

The Complaynt of Scotland (1549)

*

If the eating of Turds would come into fashion,
One Scotchman might then feed the whole English
Nation.

Eighteenth-century English quip

*

A greedy, dark, degenerate place of Sin
For th' Universe to shoot her rubbish in . . .

Pimps, Bullies, Traitors, Robbers, 'tis all one,
Scotland, like wide-jaw'd Hell, refuses none.

Anonymous, from A Trip Lately to Scotland *(1705)*

*

The Scots are like dung – no good unless spread.

Old saying quoted by Alastair Reid in the New Yorker *(1964)*

*

Why do we always get Julians and Timothys? Let's get some Wullies in charge.

Anonymous protest against the appointment of an Englishman as director of the National Galleries, quoted in A. Cran and J. Robertson, Dictionary of Scottish Quotations *(1996)*

*

What is a Scot but an uninspired Irishman?

Anonymous remark noted in Forsyth Hardy, John Grierson's Scotland *(1979)*

*

Except in Scotland.

Phrase found throughout D. Elliston Allen, British Tastes: Likes and Dislikes of the Regional Consumer *(1968)*

*

The Scotch are not that civil and polite people they are represented to be; if they are fawning, it is only to bite you – they are excellent Flatterers.

Peter Barber, Journey in Scotland, *1795*

*

The Scots are an Awful Retribution. They are to the English what the English are to the Continent. They just have a natural consciousness of their own superiority. And because they take it so for granted, the English have an uneasy sneaking sort of feeling that there may be something in it.

Theodora Benson and Betty Askwith, Foreigners *(1936)*

*

Up amid the swells of London,
Mid the pomp of purple sinners,
Where many a kilted thane was undone,
With dice, debauchery, and dinners.

John Stuart Blackie (1809–1895)

*

The devellysche dysposicion of a Scottis man, not to love nor favour an Englis man . . . Trust yow no Skott.

Andrew Boorde, English agent, letter to Thomas Cromwell, 1536

*

The great Englishman is always a lunatic with a strongly practical side.

James Bridie, A Small Stir

*

Yes, sir, the Englishman is amiable. He is the mildest mannered man ever to have scuttled ship or cut a throat.

James Bridie, *A Small Stir*

*

The darling object of the English was to subjugate the

Scotch; and if anything could increase the disgrace of so base an enterprise, it would be that, having undertaken it, they ignominiously failed.

Henry Thomas Buckle, History of Civilization in England, *Vol. III (1857)*

*

. . . for the most part the worst instructed, and the least knowing of their rank, I ever went amongst.

Gilbert Burnet (1643–1715), History of His Own Times, *on the English aristocracy*

*

Thirty millions, mostly fools.

Thomas Carlyle (1795–1881), when asked what the population of England was

*

They're Citizens o' th' World; they're all in all,
Scotland's a Nation epidemicall.

John Cleveland (1613–58), The Rebell Scot

*

First Younger Sister to the Frozen Zone,
Battered by Parent Nature's constant Frown,
Adept to Hardships, and cut out for Toil;
The best worst Climate and the worst best Soil.

Daniel Defoe (1660–1731), Caledonia

*

The Englishman remains everlastingly adolescent.

Norman Douglas (1868–1952), Old Calabria

subsidy junkies

The London Evening Standard, *1987, quoted in Maurice Smith,*
Paper Lions: the Scottish Press and National Identity *(1994)*

*

. . . the foul hordes of Scots and Picts like dark throngs of
worms . . . a set of bloody freebooters, with more hair on
their thievish faces than clothes to cover their nakedness.

Gildas (c. 493–570), De Excidio et Conquestu Britanniae,
on the Picts, from Latin

*

An Englishman is a man who lives on an island in the North
Sea governed by Scotsmen.

Philip Guedalla, Supers and Supermen *(1920)*

*

I have never hated the English, though I have frequently
pitied them. A people who have so frequently been
conquered is to be pitied, but that is another matter. They
have this saving grace, however, when they come among

us. They train easily and civilise very quickly, most of them, anyway. But gang warily when you get under an Englishman's skin. Before you get very deep you reach a thick layer of woad.

Ian Hamilton, The Taking of the Stone of Destiny *(new ed., 1991)*

*

. . . if one will only read the anecdotes of village 'loonies' with which Scots literature abounds . . . he will find that the average Scots idiot was a creature of considerably more humour than the average Englishman.

J. A. Hammerton, J. M. Barrie and His Books

*

I should hardly call a Scotchman *conceited*, though there is often something that borders strongly on the appearance of it. He has (speaking in the lump) no personal or individual pretensions. He is not proud of himself, but of being a Scotchman . . . there is perhaps a natural hardness and want of sensibility about the Scotch, which renders them (rules and the consideration of consequences apart) not very nice or scrupulous in their proceedings. . . Their impudence is extreme, their malice is cold-blooded, covert, crawling, deliberate, without the frailty or excuse of passion. . . of all *blackguards* . . . a Scotch blackguard is the worst.

William Hazlitt (1778–1830), On the Scotch Character

*

Scotland is of all other countries in the world, perhaps the one in which the question 'What is the use of that?' is most often asked.

William Hazlitt

*

The Barbarians who inhabit the banks of the Thames

David Hume (1711–1776), letter to Hugh Blair, April 1764

*

I am delighted to see the daily and hourly progress of Madness and Folly and Wickedness in England. The Consummation of these Qualities are the true Ingredients for making a fine Narrative in History, especially if followed by some signal and ruinous Convulsion, – as I hope will soon be the Case with that pernicious People.

David Hume, Letters, 1769

*

Sir, it is not so much to be lamented that Old England is lost, as that the Scotch have found it.

Samuel Johnson (1709–1784), to James Boswell, 15 May 1776

*

The people are proud, arrogant, vain-glorious boasters, bloody, barbarous and inhuman butchers. Couzenage and theft is in perfection among them, and they are perfect English-haters, they show their pride in exalting themselves, and depressing their neighbours.

Thomas Kirke, A Modern Account of Scotland by an English Gentleman *(1679)*

*

In all my travels I never met with any one Scotchman but what was a man of sense. I believe everybody of that country that has any, leaves it as fast as they can.

Dr Francis Lockier

*

Since the Union with England, Scotland's has been simply the role of caterpillar-grub stung into immobility by devouring wasp.

Hugh MacDiarmid, Lucky Poet

To an Englishman something is what it is called: to a Scotsman, something is what it is.

Sir Compton Mackenzie (1883–1972)

*

Despite everything I may say about the arrogance, tactlessness and insensitivity of the English . . . I can't help liking them.

Moray McLaren, A Small Stir

*

Boswell was praising the English highly, and saying they were a fine, open people. 'Oh –,' said Macpherson, 'an open people! their mouths, indeed, are open to gluttony to fill their belly, but I know of no other openness they have.'

James Macpherson (1734–1796), quoted in Charles Rogers, Boswelliana *(1874)*

*

A Scotsman . . . does not thank you if you call him an Englishman

George Orwell (1903–50), The Lion and the Unicorn

*

The English! My God, they ruffle my feathers. They strut this earth like medieval popes. They behave as if God has granted them divine right to be smug. We've fought their wars for them, colonized the world for them, propped up their rotten empire, and cleaned up the middens they've left behind from Belfast to Borneo. And in Whitehall and Westminster and all along their corridors of power they treat us as if we were savages, still painted in woad. A subject race of congenital idiots, a nation of Harry Lauders with curly sticks and wee daft dugs, and stags at bay, and flying haggises and tartan dollies and Annie Lauries and hoots mon Jock McKay ye'll be a' richt the nicht if ye can houghmagandie backwards.

W. Gordon Smith, Jock

*

I think, for my part, one half the nation is mad – and I find the other not very sound.

Tobias Smollett, The Adventures of Launcelot Greaves

*

England has always seemed to me to be like a grand long-distance train. A few people sit in the first-class carriages, and have first rights to the dining-car. A great many more sit in the third-class carriages and buy pork pies in the buffet-car, or bring their own sandwiches. A few hard-working fellows, shovelling coal, operating signals, applying brakes or regulator, keep the whole rattling affair moving. It is travelling quite fast, with great smoke and clatter. But where it is going is anyone's guess, except that it is definitely not the 'Flying Scotsman'.

J.D. Sutherland, Thoughts Along a Single Track

*

Scotland seems, indeed, the natural *foyer* of rebellion, as Egypt is of the plague.

John Wilkes (1727–97), to the House of Commons

*

It is of Inglis natioune
The common kind conditioune
Of Trewis the wertu to forget,   [truth]   [virtue]
And rekles of gud Faith to be.

Andrew of Wintoun (c. 1350–c. 1424), Orygynalle Cronykil of Scotland

OUT OF THE MOUTHS OF BABES

There was, and still is, a big difference in the development of national self-awareness of Scottish and English children. As young English children learn the account of their country's history, they discover the wives of Henry VIII, Armada, Empire, the Industrial Revolution. As presented, it is an open, expansive, positive story. Apart from the Union of the Crowns, and the Union of the Parliaments, Scotland plays little part in it compared with France, Spain and Holland. When young Scots come to discover the facts of their country's history, the huge part played by England makes a deep impression, and not a favourable one. Two writers have articulated this moment of realisation very clearly, on behalf of many others. The first is Robert Burns, in an autobiographical letter:

The story of Wallace poured a Scottish prejudice in my veins which will boil along there till the floodgates of life shut in eternal rest.

The second is Hugh Miller, whose sense of national belonging was also awakened by 'Blind Harry's' *Wallace*:

I first became thoroughly a Scot in my tenth year; and the consciousness of country has remained tolerably strong within me ever since . . . I was intoxicated with the fiery narrative of the blind minstrel, with his fierce breathings of hot, intolerant patriotism, and his stories of astonishing prowess; and, glorying in being a Scot, and the countryman of Wallace and the Graham, I longed for a war with the Southron, that the wrongs and sufferings of these noble heroes might yet be avenged.

Nor was it just boys who felt this passion:

In our play-hours we amused ourselves with playing at ball, marbles, and especially at 'Scotch and English', a game which represented a raid on the debatable land, or Border between Scotland and England, in which each party tried to rob the other of their playthings. The little ones were always compelled to be English, for the bigger girls thought it was too degrading.

Mary Somerville (1780–1872), Personal Recollections from Early Life in Old Age

The twentieth-century Scottish children's writer Lavinia Derwent, who grew up very near the Border, recalled a similar attitude from her own childhood: 'Only a stone's throw away lay a strange foreign country – England! I was told the natives were an unfriendly lot. Indeed they were our bitterest enemies, waiting for an opportunity to slink across the Border, steal our cattle and sheep, and burn down our abbeys . . .' When the young Lavinia went to school, as a 'Mixed Infant', she met an English girl: 'my first foreigner . . . I fought the battle bravely, but lost. The result: my first black eye, which I richly deserved. I was quite proud of it for a time, and then a strange thing happened. We became firm friends.'

This strong sense of nationality could make life difficult for English children who were brought to Scotland. The nineteenth-century writer George Borrow recalled his first Edinburgh schooldays in *Lavengro*:

'Scotland is a better country than England,' said an ugly, blear-eyed boy, about a head and shoulders taller than myself, the leader of a gang of varlets who surrounded me in the play-ground, on the first day, as soon as the morning lesson was over. 'Scotland is a far better country than England, in every respect.'

'Is it?' said I. 'Then you ought to be very thankful for not having been born in England.'

'That's just what I am, ye loon; and every morning, when I say my prayers, I thank God for not being an Englishman. The Scotch are a much better and braver people than the English.'

'It may be so,' said I, 'for what I know – indeed, till I came here, I never heard a word either about the Scotch or their country.'

'Are ye making fun of us, ye English puppy?' said the blear-eyed lad; 'take that!' and I was presently beaten black and blue. And thus did I first become aware of the difference of races and their antipathy to each other.

'Bow to the storm, and it shall pass over you.' I held my peace, and silently submitted to the superiority of the Scotch, *in numbers*. This was enough; from an object of persecution I soon became one of patronage, especially among the champions of the class.

'The English,' said the blear-eyed lad, 'though a wee bit behind the Scotch in strength and fortitude, are nae to be sneezed at, being far ahead of the Irish, to say nothing of the French, a pack of scoundrels. And with regard to the English country, it is na Scotland, it is true, but it has its gude properties; and, though there is ne'er a haggis in a' the land, there's an unco deal o' gowd and siller. I respect England, for I have an auntie married there.'

Trevor Royle experienced the conflicting pressures on an English boy growing up in Scotland during the 1950s: 'I had learned enough to get by and to survive and, more importantly from a child's point of view, to merge into the background. I remained on the outside . . . I could never (and this *was* a test) feel the intense dismay and dislike of the English that my friends felt. And why should I, being one myself? . . . When we were in Scotland we were unmistakably English, but in the South the mantle of the Scot was thrust upon us. Despite our surnames we were 'Scotties' or 'Jocks' and people smiled at the way we rolled our 'r's (how I tired of that sly joke). After a week or two we became more Scottish than the Scots and in the absence of critical countrymen boasted about our adopted country's superiority.'

THE SCOTS IN ENGLAND

A curious set of incidents occurred in 1618 when a Scot, Thomas Ross, fixed a thesis to the door of St Mary's Church, Oxford. Written in Latin, the text (now lost) recommended that all Scotsmen resident in England, with the exception of the king, his son, and a very few others, should be sent back to their homeland. This proposal for repatriation became notorious, and Ross was sent back to Scotland himself, to be tried by the High Court in Edinburgh – although he had committed no offence in Scotland – for his 'villanious and infamous Pasquell or Thesis, and damnable appendices subjoined thairto'.

Without being able to read the original, we cannot know whether the author's intention was satirical in some way, or whether he felt that his fellow-expatriates should be sent home to be safe from the fleshpots of England. Perhaps to his surprise, he was sentenced to have his right hand cut off, followed by his head. On 10 September 1618 the execution duly took place; his head was put on a spike at the Netherbow, his hand at the West Port, of Edinburgh.

*

They beg our lands, our goods, our lives,
They switch our nobles, and lye with their wives;
They pinch our gentry, and send for our benchers,
They stab our sergeants and pistoll our fencers.

Anonymous English comment on the Scots arriving in London with King James VI and I.

*

A young Scottish civil servant, working in St Andrew's House in Edinburgh, was sent down to London to represent his department at a number of meetings. It was his first visit to Whitehall. When he returned to Edinburgh, his colleagues quizzed him about his experiences.

'And what did you think about the English?' asked one, eventually.

'The English? I never met any,' said the young man. 'I only spoke to Heads of Departments.'

*

A London-dwelling Scot met a friend one day, who noticed his long face.

'What's the matter, Mungo?'

'Well, I was on jury service, and I was given three days in jail.'

'For being on a jury? How did that happen?'

'The judge said "What is your name?" and I said "Mungo Hamish MacTaggart." He said "Are you Scottish, by any chance?" and I said "Are you a bloody comedian?"'

*

The influx of Scots to England, especially London, in the eighteenth century, was noted by satirical writers, as in this anonymous verse:

> See how they press to cross the Tweed,
> And strain their limbs with eager speed!
> While Scotland from her fertile shore
> Cries, 'On my sons, return no more.'
> Hither they race with willing mind,
> Nor cast one longing look behind.

In the 1760s, a Scottish peer, Lord Bute, became prime minister. He owed the position to the fact that he was a favourite of King George III – something that did not endear him to the many English. who thought, in the words of one of their later versifiers that 'King George the Third/Ought never to have occurred'. The anti-Scottish publication *The North Briton* objected to him on principle:

The first is, that he is a *Scot* . . . I am certain, that reason could never believe that a *Scot* was fit to have management of English affairs . . . A Scot hath no more right to preferment in England than a *Hanoverian* or a *Hottentot*.

They also objected to his finding positions and sinecures for other Scots. In 1762 an anonymous diatribe entitled *A*

British Antidote to Caledonian Poison appeared, satirising the Scottish influx and Bute's jobs-for-the-boys:

Sister Peg, our ancient friend
Sends Mac's and Donalds without end.

This, incidentally, seems to be the earliest reference to Scots as 'Macs'. A braver poet, Charles Churchill (1731–64) put his name to *The Prophecy of Famine*, a satirical poem on the Scottish influx. It mocks the Scots' pretension to being all of noble blood, like his shepherd-boy heroes, Jocky and Sawney, 'Whose birth beyond all question springs/From great and glorious, though forgotten, kings.' Another Scots boast, that the Romans had never conquered their country, was also dealt with; Famine, foster-mother of all Scots, is made to say:

Lang free, because the race of Roman braves
Thought it not worth their while to make us slaves.

THE ENGLISH IN SCOTLAND

In the bar lounge of an Aberdeen hotel, a group of English businessmen were relaxing, and discussing the reputation of the city in which they found themselves. Realising that the people at the next table were locals, one of them leaned across to the nearest man and said:

'I say, old chap, can you tell me the difference between an Aberdonian and a coconut?'

The man shook his head.

'Well,' said the Englishman, 'you can get a drink out of a coconut.'

His friends collapsed in guffaws.

'Would you like a drink?' said the Aberdonian.

'That's jolly kind of you,' said the visitor.

'Away and buy yoursel' a coconut, then.'

*

Up in Sutherland, a countryman came across one of his neighbours by the roadside, crying his eyes out.

'What's the matter, Archie?' he asked.

'Oh,' sobbed his friend, 'I've just seen an English touring bus drive straight over the cliff there.'

'A desperate thing,' said the man.

'Indeed, and nearly half the seats in it were empty,' mourned Archie.

AN OBSERVER OF THE SCOTS: SYDNEY SMITH

Sydney Smith, the celebrated English clergyman and wit, spent five years in Edinburgh between 1798 and 1803. As a contributor (he was one of its founders) to the *Edinburgh Review*, he kept up the connection long after his return to England. Some of his comments on the Scots are well-known. The most famous, that 'It requires a surgical operation to get a joke well into a Scotch understanding' is a tease – Smith happily played up to Scottish susceptibilities.

Any suggestion that they had not a sense of humour was bound to make them rise. But some of his remarks are more penetrating, like: 'A Scotchman always says what is undermost.' He joins a long train of his fellow-countrymen in remarking on the smells and related hazards of Edinburgh, despite its beauties:

> Taste guides my eye, where e'er new beauties spread,
> While prudence whispers 'look before you tread'.

Smith also probed other sensitive areas:

Their temper stands anything but an attack on their climate. They would have you even believe that they can ripen fruit; and, to be candid, I must own in remarkably warm summers I have tasted peaches that made most excellent pickles; and it is upon record that at the siege of Perth, on one occasion, their ammunition failing, their nectarines made admirable cannon balls.

Smith liked to picture the Scots as idealists, the English as pragmatists. In a letter to his friend John Allen, he wrote:

If you were sailing from Alicant to Aleppo in a storm, and, after the sailors had held up the image of a saint and prayed to it, the storm were to abate, you would be more sorry for the encouragement of superstition than rejoiced at the preservation of your life; and so would every other man born and bred in Edinburgh. My views of the matter would be much shorter and coarser: I should be so glad to find myself alive, that I should not care a farthing if the storm had generated a thousand new, and revived as many old saints.

AN OBSERVER OF THE ENGLISH:
A.G. MACDONNELL

One of the best-known portrayals of the English is in *England, Their England*, by a Scot, A.G. Macdonnell, first published in 1933. It is written as fiction, being the discovery of England by a young and naïve Scot who plans to write a book on 'The English Character'. Unlike *The Unspeakable Scot*, it is a kindly book, written with a light touch. Set among the literary and upper classes, it presents a limited picture, though it is striking how little – in many ways – has changed in the ensuing decades. The hero, Donald Cameron, searching for 'typical Englishmen', finds there is no such thing. Instead he encounters a nation of individuals, linked by a variety of different codes and by whom life seems to be regarded as a game played by arcane and unwritten rules. To the serious Donald, their flippancy is often mystifying, but their seriousness is equally baffling. In one episode, he has just watched a fox-hunt, in which the fox, run to earth, was dug out and killed: 'because, after all, the countryside must be saved from vermin even if ladies and gentlemen have to chase them on horseback for an hour and a half, and furthermore it would be an act of callous cruelty to dumb animals, which no Englishman could be guilty of, to deprive the sixty dogs of the midday meal which they had so bravely earned.' In its gentle way, the book points out some of the inconsistencies of the English way of life and state of mind. What comes most strongly from it is the author's sense of admiration at a country which – so unlike Scotland – feels no need to compare itself with anywhere else. All its characters share a self-sufficient serenity in their Englishness.

'We had an English subaltern once in our battery who used to run and extinguish fires in ammunition dumps . . . He said that shells cost five pounds each and it was everyone's duty to save government money.'

'Where is he buried?' asked Cameron

A.G. Macdonnell (1895–1941), England, Their England

ANGLO-SCOTTISH EXCHANGES

I wondered not, when I was told
The venal Scot his country sold;
I rather very much admire
How he could ever find a buyer.

Anonymous English verse, c. 1780

*

An English visitor to Scotland was enjoying himself by
making sarcastic remarks to some Scots about their choice
of the thistle as their national emblem. One of the Scots
replied, mildly:

'Well, it is true enough, the thistle may be the pride of the
Scottish nation, but in the mouth of an ass it is nothing.'

*

The English tourist had been fishing for a whole week on
Loch Tay without even getting a bite. Then, on the last day,
he finally hooked and landed a salmon. He looked at it a
little wryly.

'You know, Tommy,' he said to his ghillie, 'this fish has
cost me four hundred pounds.'

'Well, sir,' said Thomas, 'it's a good thing you only
caught the one.'

*

An English lawyer, in Scotland for the shooting, strayed
away from the rest of his party one morning. He had hit
nothing so far, but as he turned to rejoin them, he suddenly
saw a fine grouse flying close by. Instantly he brought up
his gun and, bang! he got it. It fell to the ground at the other
side of a fence, and as he leapt over to retrieve it, another
man came running up.

'Hey!' he shouted. 'This is my land.'

'But it's my grouse,' said the lawyer.

'No it's not. I saw you shooting over the fence.'

'Listen, friend,' said the Englishman. 'I am a lawyer specialising in property. You don't want to tangle with me or you'll find yourself in court, on the losing side, and facing the biggest bill for costs that you ever saw in your life. Get it?'

'I see,' said the farmer. 'Well, why don't we settle it country-style, man-to-man?'

'What do you mean?' asked the lawyer.

'It's a kick-and-yell contest,' said the farmer. 'We take turns to bend over and let the other fellow kick our backside. Six kicks a round. The first to yell is the loser.'

'Okay,' said the lawyer.

He was a stout, burly fellow and the other looked a light-weight by comparison. He bent over. My God, he thought, but the man can kick! It was all he could do to stop himself yelling with the pain. After the sixth he stood up, his backside aching but his eyes gleaming for revenge, and saw the other man holding out the grouse.

'I've decided you can have it, after all,' said the farmer, pleasantly.

THE UNION OF THE CROWNS

For James VI of Scotland, the death of his distant relative Elizabeth I of England provided the opportunity he had long and impatiently awaited – to become king of England (and Ireland) as well as of Scotland. James was over the moon, and very soon over the Border; but many of his Scottish subjects were less enthusiastic about his transition. One of them, William Forbes of Disblair, wrote *A Pil for Pork-Eaters: Or, A Scots Lancet for an English Swelling:*

> CURS'D be the Day (for then we were betray'd)
> When first our King the *English* Scepter sway'd.
> As never State nor Kingdom did before:
> From neighbouring States we no Assistance crav'd,
> We scorn'd by foreign Yokes to be enslav'd;
> Had Wealth at Home, Alliances Abroad;
> Yea of our Friendship *France* itself was proud;
> Each Scot was brave, with Noble Courage fir'd;
> Our Court Polite, and every where admir'd.
> Thus from a Nation full of Power and Fame,
> We're dwindl'd to a Thing, scarce worth a Name.

Dissatisfaction in Scotland was so great that James VI had an Act of Parliament passed in 1609 against 'Scandalous Speeches and Libels', forbidding the Scots to insult the English in: '... pasquillis, libellis, rymis, Cockalanis, comedies and sicklyk occasionis whereby they slander maligne and revile the estait and country of England and divers his majesties honorable Counsallors, magistratis and worthie subjectis of that his majesties kingdome'. Imprisonment, banishment, fines and 'mair rigorous Corporal pane' were all threatened against those who persisted in such un-British behaviour.

Numerous Scots came south to join the court, and the invasion, though on a small scale compared with the next century, clearly was not always well received. In 1605 three playwrights, George Chapman, Ben Jonson, and John Marston were briefly imprisoned for a rude reference to Scots in their play *Eastward Ho*. One character, Seagull, refers to the colony of Virginia as an agreeable place without any unpleasant inhabitants, except for 'a few industrious Scots perhaps, who are indeed dispersed over the face of the whole earth. But as for them there are no greater friends to England and Englishmen, when they are on't, in the world than they are. And for my own part, I would that a hundred thousand of them were there, for we are all one countrymen now, ye know, and we should find ten times as more comfort of them there than we do here.'

*

In 1700, during negotiations on a possible union, the English Sir Edward Seymour remarked that Scotland 'was a beggar, and whoever married a beggar could only expect a louse for a portion'.

The anonymous Scottish writer of *The True Scottish Genius* in 1704 described his country as:

> Bereav'd of Power, of Riches, and of Trade,
> Still slavishly to *England's* Int'rest ty'd.

TWO SHORT NOTES ON CULTURE

Englishman: Do you know why they are training Russian cosmonauts in Scotland?
Scotsman: No, why?
Englishman: Because it has absolutely no atmosphere.

*

Scot, proudly: I suppose you know that it was a Scot who developed penicillin?
Englishman: Yes, it's the only culture a Scotsman ever developed.

DRESS

In the matter of costume, the humour traffic is largely one-way, from south to north. There may be some quite bizarre forms of dress in England, like that of Morris dancers with their knotted hankies, their bells and garlands, but Morris dancing is the pursuit of a very small number, and they are certainly not wearing the national dress. Scotland by contrast has one of the most conspicuous 'national' costumes, for males, in the world. This is not the place to go into the origins of Highland dress, apart from one thing. Some English commentators have rejoiced in pointing out that the kilt, in its present form, was invented by an Englishman, Mr Rawlinson, manager of the iron-works at Glengarry, in the 1720s, as the belted plaid was too cumbersome a garment for his Highland workers. There is great pleasure to be had in the thought that this flaunted sign of Scottishness is owed to an Englishman. It is around this time that the word 'kilt' first appears; the Gaelic form, rendered in English as 'philabeg', has no relation to it. But though Mr Rawlinson, like many a Scottish-based Englishman to follow, is said to have taken up wearing the kilt himself, there is no real evidence that he pioneered the pleated kilt design, which is more likely to have been devised by a travelling tailor. His fellow countryman Edmund Burt, in the Highlands at much the same time, makes numerous references to the 'quelt', but says nothing of its origins.

Long before that, the Highlanders in the *feille mòr* or 'great kilt' had attracted the notice of the wider world. 'Redshanks' was the usual name, in reference to their bare legs, given to them by the English in Ireland. It is doubtful if many kilted Scots reached England until the arrival of Prince Charles Edward Stuart's army in 1745. After that episode, the kilt was firmly ingrained into English consciousness as an attribute of the Scots. (Ironically, of course, it is only since 1832 and the visit of king George IV to Edinburgh, that the kilt has become 'national' – before that it was worn only by the Highlanders and regarded by

Lowland Scots as primitive and far from respectable). Lord Macaulay, commenting on George IV 'disguising himself in what, before the Union, was considered by nine Scotchmen out of ten as the dress of a thief' remarked: 'As long as the Gaelic dress was worn, the Saxons had pronounced it hideous, ridiculous, nay, grossly indecent. Soon after it had been prohibited, they discovered it was the most graceful drapery in Europe.'

Lord Mansfield, eleventh son of the earl of Stormont, born in the then somewhat ramshackle Scone castle, became the Lord Chief Justice of England. He was sent to Westminster School at the age of fourteen, but prior to that had gone to the grammar school of Perth. London's Grub Street pamphleteers liked to mock at Mansfield's early years as a kilted Scottish schoolboy: 'Learning was very cheap in his country, and it is very common to see a boy of quality lug along his books to school, and a scrap of oatmeal for his dinner, with a pair of brogues on his feet, posteriors exposed, and nothing on his legs.'

In the days when men wore knee-breeches, and fastened them at the knee with a buckle, someone developed a special patent buckle, and sued another man who had copied it. In the London court, counsel for the prosecution was the Scot Thomas Erskine, later to be Lord Chancellor. He held up the patent buckle to the jury, expatiating on its merits as a fastener. 'How would my ancestors have admired this specimen of dexterity,' he exclaimed. The opposing counsel, an Englishman, had an answer ready: 'Gentlemen,' he said to the jury, 'you have heard a good deal today of my learned friend's ancestors and their probable astonishment at his knee-buckles. But gentlemen, I can assure you, their astonishment would have been quite as great at his breeches.'

When Sydney Smith wrote about a political mob: 'did not the Scotch philosophers tear off the clothes of the Tories in Mintoshire?' he could not forbear from adding, '. . . or at least such clothes as the custom of the country admit of being worn?'

Some people have regarded Harris Tweed as a joke perpetrated against the upper-class English. The writer Finlay J. Macdonald commented on 'a highly distinctive odour of which whiffs may still, very occasionally, be detected in the corridors of the House of Lords . . . pervasively, and unmistakably to the cognoscenti, there comes through, on humid days in particular, the inter-reaction of wool and urine.' This is not, he points out, because of any incontinence among the aristocracy but goes back to the making of the tweed of their suits, when the raw wool was 'waulked' in the stale urine of the Hebridean population. But the joke can unfortunately rebound on the tweed-clad Scots themselves.

Nowadays kilt jokes remain popular outside Scotland, and their obsession with gender and sex is more blatant, even when it is not insulting:

When the good Lord made the Jocks, he did not design them to go upstairs in tramcars.

W. Gordon Smith

*

Queen Victoria, to kilted Scot: Is anything worn under the kilt?
Kilted Scot: No, ma'am, it's all in perfect working order.

(I believe this joke originated with the colonial-born Irish-Englishman Spike Milligan)

*

A nineteenth century *Punch* joke was made in a two-stage drawing.

Scene One – Cockney Tourist, to Scotsman in Highland dress, who is leaning against the wall of a bridge:

'Hey, Scotty, show us the Highland fling!'

Scene Two – The Scotsman tosses the Cockney Tourist over the bridge and into the river.

*

Question: What does a Scotsman wear under his kilt?
Answer: Socks and shoes.

*

But there are others of a cruder sort:

Why do Scotsmen wear kilts?
So that the sheep won't hear zips being undone.

FOOD AND DRINK

Neither the English nor the Scots stand high in the list of culinary nations. Both have been blasted for their indifference to good cooking and the amenities of the table. The Frenchman Faujas de St-Fond in the eighteenth century remarked that 'the English and Scotch attach no importance to the fine perfume and flavour of good coffee for it seems to be all one to them what kind they drink, provided they have four or five cupfuls'. The Neapolitan ambassador, Carraciolo, famously remarked that the English have thirty kinds of religion, but only one sauce. For that reason, perhaps, there is not a great deal of banter exchanged on food topics. The English used to enjoy the story about the hotel guest who came downstairs on his first morning in Scotland and saw porridge for the first time. He complained to the manager that someone had been sick on his plate. With a range of ethnic foods that also included haggis, the Scots provided another distinctive aspect for the English to tease. There was not much of a two-way trade here: neither country was considered to have anything to teach others about cookery. The French could, and did, mock the cooking of England; the Scots were not in a position to do this. Nevertheless, whatever the culinary and hygienic standards the English used to face at home, most of them found Scotland worse:

'I observed no Art of Cookery, or furniture of Houshold stuff, but rather rude neglect of both,' wrote the English visitor Fynes Morison in 1598.

*

'There is great store of fowl,' observed Sir Anthony Weldon, going on to commit a foul pun: 'as foul houses, foul sheets, foul linen, foul dishes and pots . . . They have good store of fish too, and good for those that can eat it raw; but if it come once into their hands, it is worse than if it were three days old: for their butter and cheese, I will not meddle withal at this time, nor no man else at any time that loves his life.'

*

'Their pewter pots, wherein they bring wine and water, are furred within, that it would loathe you to touch anything that comes out of them', shuddered Sir William Brereton in 1636. 'To come into their kitchen, and see them dress their meat, and to behold the sink (which is more offensive than any jakes) will be a sufficient supper, and will take off the edge of your stomach.'

*

Thomas Kirke echoed his words forty-three years later: 'To put one's head into their kitchen doors is little less than destructive; you enter Hell alive, where the black furies are busy in mangling dead carcases and the fire and brimstone, or rather stew and stink, is ready to suffocate you . . .'

*

When Edmund Burt visited Edinburgh in 1725, he had already encountered the Scots' notion of hygiene at Kelso, but still: 'the cook was too filthy an object to be described; only another English gentleman whispered me and said, he believed, if the fellow was to be thrown against the wall, he would stick to it.'

*

Very occasionally, a Scot has felt sufficient confidence to denigrate English cooking:

Even a boiled egg tastes of mutton fat in England.

Norman Douglas, Old Calabria

*

Of haggis, now so closely associated with Scotland, it must be said that it is first found mentioned in England, in the *Liber Cocorum*, or Book of Cooks, one of the earliest cookbooks. That was in 1402; and there is evidence from other writings, culinary and otherwise, that the haggis remained a popular dish there for several centuries. One of the comic characters in Ben Jonson's seventeenth-century play *Bartholomew Fair* is 'Haggis – a watchman'. Haggis is no Scottish immigrant but a pure cockney. It seems likely that haggis declined in England, its demise spreading northwards. But in Scotland, it kept its popularity. In this respect, as with bagpipe music, Scotland preserved a worthy old European custom which the fashions of richer and trendier countries disdained.

A Sotsman died, and duly presented himself at the entrance gate of Heaven.

'Have you led a good and blameless life?' said St Peter.

'I have.'

'What is your name?' said St Peter.

'Archibald MacNab.'

'Are you Scottish by any chance?'

'Indeed I am.'

'Then you can't come in. We're not making haggis for one.'

*

Of Scots ale, Richard Franck remarked in 1656, 'so thick and roapy it was, you might eat it with spoons.'

*

The Scots were greater drinkers than the English, and frequently had better wine: no visitors complained about the quality of their claret. Even Scots admitted the English were more temperate. When James Hogg, author of *Confessions of a Justified Sinner*, went to London in 1832, he wrote to his wife: 'The people here are all sober there being no deep drinking here as in Scotland . . . I have not seen one drunk person neither poor not rich.'

*

A Scottish climber was high up in the Alps with a friend from England when they both were caught in a snow slide. Luckily it was a small one, and, though bruised and battered, they were able to cling to some rocks and wait for a rescue party to arrive. The first sign of rescue was a huge St Bernard dog that loomed up out of the snow, the traditional barrel of brandy tucked under its chin.

'Ah, look, Man's best friend,' said the Englishman.

'Yes,' said the Scotsman enthusiastically, 'and look at the size of the dog that's carrying it.'

A STUSHIE BETWEEN HISTORIANS

It is not only in sport that latter-day rivalries and spats break out between Scotland and England. A notable joust took place in the 1970s when the Scottish historian William Ferguson assailed the English historian Hugh Trevor-Roper.

With phrases like 'Perhaps sometime they [Trevor-Roper and his followers] should descend from their airy theoretical heights to dart a glance at the evidence', Trevor-

Roper's thoughts on the Scottish Reformation are dismissed by Ferguson as 'a mish-mash of elementary points, none too accurately handled, strung together with rhetorical questions and garnished with burlesque humour. In his excursions into "Scotch history" he is very unkind to himself . . . With his information so limited and his method of argument so defective, it is to be feared that Trevor-Roper's celebrated essay on "Scotland and the Puritan Revolution" contains more to admire at than to admire.'

A reader of the essay can certainly detect a patronising tone. When Trevor-Roper refers to English historians' view of seventeenth-century Scotland as 'a barbarous country populated only by doltish peasants manipulated, for their own factious ends, by ambitious noblemen and fanatical ministers', one senses that he has some sympathy with it. But what got up Tevor-Roper's nose was the patronising approach of the 'fanatical ministers' from Scotland. That such persons should come to England and presume to interfere with its ordering of religious practice seems to have offended him deeply, and he writes with waspish spite of such characters as Robert Baillie (admittedly a religious bigot of insufferable complacency, but it was three hundred years ago), and compares the reactions to London of one Presbyterian, Alexander Brodie, to those of a Bedouin transported to the splendours of Baghdad.

HYGIENE

The Scotch seem to be an improving People; but I am sorry to say their Shitteries are in a state of Barbarism. . . the many Daubs upon the Wall, the Condition of the *Seat*, and the intolerable Stench issuing from it, will be an eternal reflection upon the North.

Peter Barber, Journey in Scotland, *1795*

THE INTOLERABLE SENSE OF SUPERIORITY OF THE ENGLISH

The tone adopted by Professor Trevor-Roper (later Lord Dacre) in his ruminations on Scotland was not a new one. It was in the sixteenth century that English complacency really began to be expressed. William Harrison, in his *Description of England* (1577), wrote that the English are 'blessed in every waie, and there is temporall commoditie necessarie to be had or craved by any nation at God's hand that he hath not in most abundant manner bestowed on us Englishmen'.

In the next century, John Milton wrote: 'It is in God's manner to reveal Himself first to his Englishmen.' From such a thought it was but a short step to the 'God is an Englishman' view. As the English writer Paul Langford notes, of other peoples' view of the English: 'They assumed that what drove them was a unique, or at any rate insular, sense of destiny based more on arrogance than moral superiority. The essence of the claim was not so much that the English reasoned that they were superior to others but that it genuinely did not occur to them that any rational being could suppose they were anything else . . . To be born an Englishman implied an act of divine grace that left its beneficiaries profoundly grateful.'

*

'Remember that you are an Englishman and have consequently won first prize in the lottery of life.'

Cecil Rhodes (1853–1902)

THE INTOLERABLE SENSE OF SUPERIORITY OF THE SCOTS

Minds like ours, my dear James, must always be above national prejudices, and in all companies it gives me true pleasure to declare that, as a people, the English are very little indeed inferior to the Scotch.

Christopher North (John Wilson, 1785–1854), Blackwood's Magazine

*

The Scots have always been famed for their dignified humility. They know themselves to be perfervidly ingenious and to be the admiration and envy of all other peoples. It would be most shocking if they were addicted to rubbing it in. They can be tolerant of and even amused at the Englishman's pretensions to having a Scottish great-grandmother.

James Bridie

*

Oddly enough they are always brought up with a jerk, and resent it when we treat them as foreigners, when we submit their peculiarities to laughter or applaud their virtues as something rich and strange.

Moray McLaren

MR BOSWELL'S BEAR

Perhaps the most articulate of all Scottophobes was Dr Samuel Johnson (1709–84). But, oddly, Johnson's anti-Scots pronouncements have only been preserved through the obsessive attention of his Scottish friend and biographer, James Boswell, who insisted that the great Englishman was not anti-Scottish at all. Boswell (1740–85) was convinced that Johnson's famous animosity to the Scots was caused by his reaction to the Scots' own nationalistic fervour. He quotes Johnson as saying to an acquaintance: 'When I find a Scotchman, to whom an Englishman is as a Scotchman, that Scotchman shall be as an Englishman to me.' Yet he was also obliged to admit that Johnson 'considered the Scotch, nationally, as a crafty, designing people, eagerly attentive to their own interest, and too apt to overlook the claims and pretentions of other people'.

More than most London Scots of the eighteenth century, Boswell suffered from a confused sense of national identity. His instincts and most of his attitudes were Scottish: his inclinations were English. He was one of those who tried vainly to establish the common term 'Briton', with its 'North' and 'South' division. A faithful if sometimes inadvertent chronicler of his own failings, Boswell has never been quite forgiven by his compatriots for his self-revelation in his very first conversation with Johnson:

Boswell: I do indeed come from Scotland, but I cannot help it.
Johnson: That, Sir, I find, is what a very great many of your countrymen cannot help.

This first exchange set the tone for many subsequent Johnsonian gibes:

'The noblest prospect which a Scotchman ever sees is the high road that leads him to England.'

'We have taught you (said he) and we'll do the same in time towards all barbarous nations, – to the Cherokee –, and at last to the Orang-Outangs.'

'Much may be made of a Scotchman, if he be caught young.'

'Your country consists of two things, stone and water. There is, indeed, a little earth above the stone in some places, but a very little, and the stone is always appearing. It is like a man in rags; the naked skin is still peeping out.'

Often Johnson was merely baiting his friend by his comments, but his fundamental disapproval of the Scots does appear to rest on what he called their 'extreme nationality': their clannishness and mutual support – based not on personal merit but merely on being fellow-Scots. Even on his celebrated visit to Scotland, he did not hesitate to take issue with them, as in his riposte to a critic of the Union with England:

James Kerr: Half our nation was bribed by English money.
Dr Johnson: Sir, that is no defence. It makes you worse.

Many Scots were determined not to seem too impressed by their distinguished visitor. The writer Henry Mackenzie noted that: 'When Boswell was bear-leading Johnson through Scotland, he introduced him, in the Parliament House at Edinburgh, to Henry Erskine, who, after making his bow and a short conversation left the conductor and conducted, putting a shilling into Boswell's hand, being the common fee for a sight of wild beasts.'

JUNGLE TALE

A Scotsman and an Englishman were tramping along a jungle path together. Suddenly they came to a clearing. At the other side was a huge tiger, crouched, ready to spring. Immediately the Scotsman sat down, pulled off his heavy boots, and got a pair of running shoes out of his backpack.

'What's the use?' said the Englishman. 'You'll never outrun it.'

'No,' said the Scotsman, 'but I'll outrun you.'

LITERARY FLURRIES

When Robert Henryson's Animal Fables were first published in England, in 1577, as *The Fabulous Tales of Esope the Phrygian*, they were advertised as translated: 'Compiled moste eloquently in Scottisch Metre . . . and now lately Englished'. Their translator, Richard Smith, notes the neglect of Scottish literature in England, and puts it down to political reasons, which he seems to share:

But whether most men have that nation in derision for their hollowe hearts and ungratefull mindes to this country alwayes had (a people verie subject to that infection) or thinking scorne of the Authour or first inventor let it passe.

– he doesn't care much, anyway. In the Prologue, written by himself, Smith makes Aesop-Henryson say of the English:

They do not vare for Scottish bookes,
They list not looke that way:
But if they would but cast their lookes
Some time when thy do play,
Somewhat to see perhaps they might
That then would like them wel,
To teach then treade thair way aright
To blisse, from paines of hel.

*

The English poet John Skelton (*see* Old Wars section) attacked a Scot, Sir George Dundas, who had written a Latin poem reminding the world that Englishmen had tails.

Part of his diatribe reads:

> Skelton laureat
> After this rate
> Defendeth with his pen
> All Englysh men
> Agayn Dundas
> That Scottishe asse
>
> Dundas, dronken and drowsy
> Skabed, scurvy and lowsy,
> Of unhappy generacion
> And most ungracious nacion.

*

It is said that a Scotchman returning home after some years' residence in England, being asked what he thought of the English, answered: 'They hanna ower muckle sense, but they are an unco braw people to live amang;' which would be a very good story, if it were not rendered apocryphal, by the incredible circumstance of the Scotchman going back.

Thomas Love Peacock (1785–1866), Crotchet Castle

LONDON SCOTS

The London Scot has always had a bad press. Usually viewed as male, he is the archetype of the Scotsman on the make – ambitious and none too scrupulous. In the eighteenth century, their chief critic was the English poet Charles Churchill, who comments on the preference given to his Scottish rival-versifiers by Lord Bute, as king's adviser and later prime minister:

> These simple bards, by simple prudence taught,
> To this wise town by simple patrons brought,

In simple manner utter simple lays,
And take, with simple pensions, simple praise.

For these Scots, England awaits:

For us, the Earth shall bring forth her increase,
For us, the Flocks shall wear a Golden Fleece;
For Beeves shall yield us dainties not our own,
And the Grape shall bleed a nectar yet unknown,
For our advantage shall their Harvests grow,
And Scotsmen reap, what they disdained to sow.

*

The Scot ... is often uncouth enough in his native land. When he goes to London, he is usually intolerable ... the London Scot is an ill-mannered and pretentious oaf and exactly the man to slap you on the back at one moment and kick you downstairs the next.

James Bridie

LORDS A-LEAPING

Among the *Roxburgh Ballads* is preserved 'The Leaping of the Lords', an account in verse of an unusual challenge. Three Scottish lords challenged the lords of England to a jumping competition. The stake was £7000 – a vast amount of money – and the contest took place before King James and his son, the future Charles I. The English champion, the earl of Southampton, was the winner, clearing a distance of 'six yards and full two foot' – a twenty-foot leap, not bad for a man who must have been in his late thirties. The king teased him, saying he made an even bigger jump from the Tower of London (James had freed him from the Tower in 1603). Lord Derby interposed to say: 'Your Grace did more

– you leapt a greater leap from Scotland's gate to wear our English crown.'

MORE OBSERVERS OF THE ENGLISH –
A SMALL STIR

In 1949, two well-known literary Scots, Moray McLaren and James Bridie (pen-name of Osborne Henry Mavor), published a collected exchange of letters under this name. Subtitled 'Letters on the English', it is based on the supposed fact that 'the English take ten times more trouble to understand their neighbours than their neighbours do to understand them', and that it is time to redress the balance. Various aspects of Englishness are examined through a Scottish prism. There are some good things in the letters, though the authors are somewhat too self-regarding, there is an occasional whiff of the sort of bovine facetiousness of 'Christopher North' in *Blackwood's Magazine*, and in their striving to display a somewhat un-Scottish urbanity of manner, both writers show they are writing primarily for an English audience. It is rather a pity that someone like Hugh MacDiarmid ('hobby: Anglophobia' said his entry in *Who's Who*) was not included in the correspondence.

MUSIC

Once upon a time the bagpipe was the most common musical instrument in Europe. Its materials were readily available and it was cheap to make. Providing the player with an extra lung, it was able to produce sustained sound, and its range could encompass the wedding dance, the funeral lament and the battle charge. But by the end of the Middle Ages, the bagpipe had become obsolete almost everywhere in western Europe except Scotland. The Scots not only kept it but developed a new form of music for it, the *pibroch*.

English rudeness about the bagpipes is not new:

'Musick they have, but not the harmony of the sphears, but loud terrene noises, like the bellowing of beasts; the loud bagpipe is their chief delight.'

Thomas Kirke, A Modern Account of Scotland *(1679)*

The pipes, like all unusual and distinctive musical instruments, suffer from the rash of one-dimensional internet-type jokes.

What's the difference between a bagpipe and an onion?
No-one cries when you chop up a bagpipe.

*

How do you get two pipers to play in unison?
Shoot one of them.

*

Definition of a gentleman: someone who knows how to

play the bagpipes – and doesn't.

*

Did you hear about the piper who left his pipes lying on the back seat of his car? Someone broke the window and left another set of pipes alongside them.

*

But the pipes have the last word. As W. Gordon Smith noted, they are also: '. . . terror in the hearts of the enemy. The greatest laxative in the world.'

*

'The English are a funny people,' remarked Hamish, on his return from a holiday south of the Border. 'I was in my hotel room one night, walking up and down, playing a few tunes on the pipes, and someone came hammering on the door and shouted "Make less noise!"'

'What did you do?' asked his friend.

'I took my boots off,' said Hamish.

The Scots have not mocked at any musical tradition preserved by the English, though they may have searched to find one.

NAME-CALLING

At Babel names from pride and discord flowed;
And ever since men with a female spite
First call each other names, and then they fight.
Scotland and England! Cause of just uproar,
Do man and wife signify rogue and whore?

Andrew Marvell (1621–78), The Loyal Scot

John Bull and Sister Peg

Dr John Arbuthnot (1667–1735) was a witty medical man who had a taste for literature and the literary life, and who hailed originally from Arbuthnott, Kincardineshire, where his father had been the Episcopalian parson. He was a long-time resident of London, and it was in 1712 that he created the persona of 'John Bull' to represent the typical Englishman, in *The Famous History of John Bull,* part of a series of satires written against the duke of Marlborough, Arbuthnot drew a comparison between John Bull and his sister, 'poor Peg' (Peg being short for Margaret, at that time the most usual female name in Scotland):

John Bull in the main was an honest plain-dealing fellow, choleric, bold, and of a very inconstant temper. He dreaded not old Lewis [France] . . . but then he was very apt to quarrel with his best friends, especially if they pretended to govern him. If you flattered him, you might lead him as a child.

John Bull, otherwise a good-natured man, was very hard-hearted to his sister Peg, chiefly from an aversion he had conceived in his infancy. While he flourished, kept a warm house, and drove a plentiful trade, poor Peg was forced to go hawking and peddling about the streets, and when she could not get bread for her family, she was forced to hire them out at journey-work to her neighbours. Yet in these poor circumstances she still preserved the air and mien of a gentlewoman, a certain decent pride, that extorted respect from the haughtiest of her neighbours; when she came in to any assembly, she would not yield the *pas* to the best of them. If one asked her, 'Are you related to John Bull?' 'Yes,' says she, 'he has the honour to be my brother.'

Arbuthnot's view was a kindly one, as might befit one of the first 'Anglo-Scots', a physician-in-ordinary to Queen Anne, and a user of Augustan English prose who probably never wrote a word of Scots in his life. 'Sister Peg' did not however catch on for Scotland, though one or two writers use the term. Scotland already had a female persona in Caledonia. Anglia never took human shape: clearly any sort of feminine identity for the land of roast beef lacked conviction. Britannia, though familiar as a buxom lady sitting by a union-jack cheese – and, in *Rule Britannia*, saluted by a Scotsman, James Thomson – has remained a glacial, imperial figure devoid of personality.

Strangely enough, neither the Scots nor the English have a special derogatory term that applies to the other nation. With their strong sense of culinary conservatism, the English called the French 'Frogs' on account of their supposed eating habits. Germans, Italians, and Spaniards were also favoured with special terms. The French retaliated at one time by calling the English 'les goddams', after the English soldiery's favourite epithet. But between Scotland and England, the blood was often bad enough for the mere word 'Scot' to be a term of abuse. By the eighteenth century, 'Scotch' was taking on a tinge of offensiveness south of the border, which is why it has also dropped out of use to the north, except in one or two phrases.

The Scottish word 'Sassenach', nowadays cheerfully used in a jokingly self-apologetic way by the English; has lost its sting in use for the Scots. Its original Gaelic form simply means 'Saxon'. But as most comments on the Saxon were in a context of complaint, insult or mockery, it acquired the same sort of taint as 'Scotch' did. 'Southron', the word used for English in Blind Harry's *Wallace*, also clearly had the same derogatory sense.

But just 'English' can be enough. In John Buchan's romance *Huntingtower*, the Scottish hero, Dickson McCunn, feels obliged to explain to an old lady the curious behaviour of his English ally, John Heritage: 'English', he says, significantly. No more needs to be said.

*

I am glad to see you make a point of calling them 'Scotchmen' not 'Scotsmen' as they like to be called. I find this a good easy way of annoying them.

George Orwell, letter to Anthony Powell (1936)

OLD WARS, AND BATTLES LONG AGO

Invasion and warfare are invariably accompanied by a propaganda campaign, and usually followed up by rancour and anger on the part of the losers. The oldest traceable records of such exchanges between Scotland and England go back to the time of Edward I and Robert Bruce. An anonymous poet writing in Latin made the boast: *Unus Anglus perimet Scoticos quam plures* – 'One Englishman is worth many Scots', and another compared the Scots' struggle against Edward I to that of a pig rebelling against a lion:

Quasi sus insurgeret leonis virtuti,
Sic expugnant Angliam Scotici polluti

'As a pig might rise up against the splendour of the lion, so the dirty Scots fight against England.'

*

The patriotic English poet Laurence Minot has left a number of poems attacking the Scots, some of which hark back to events before his birth in 1333. In this he warns the traitorous Scots and their French allies not to mess with Edward Longshanks:

The traytours of Scotlond token hem to rede
                            [take counsel]
The barouns of engeland to brynge to dede;
                            [to do to death]
Charles of fraunce, so mani men tolde,
with myht & with streynthe hem helpe wolde
                            [would help them]
his thonkes!   [thanks to him!]
Tprot, Scot, for this strif!   [strife]
Hang up thyn hachet and thi knyfe,
                            [while he with the long
                                shanks lives]
Whil him lasteth the lyf,
With the longe shonkes.

*

Following the Scottish victory at Bannockburn in 1314, an anonymous Scots bard jeered:

Maydens of Englande, sore may ye morne
For your lemmans ye have lost at Bannockysborne,
                            [lovers]
With heve a lowe.

What, weneth the kynge of Englande   [thinks]
So soone to have wonne Scotlande?

*

After the English victory over the invading Scots at Halidon
Hill in 1333, an equally anonymous versifier was able to hit
back:

> Scots out of Berwick and out of Aberdeen,
> At the burn of Bannock ye were far too keen.
> Many guiltless men ye slew, as was clearly seen,
> But King Edward has avenged it now, and fully too, I
> ween.

– and again:

> 'Tis now, thou rough-foot, brogue-clad Scot, that begins
> thy care,
> Thou boastful barley-bag-man, thy dwelling is all bare.
> False wretch and forsworn, whither wilt thou fare?

*

Blind Harry, the fifteenth-century poet who composed *The
Wallace*, was bitterly anti-English – not surprisingly,
considering the fate meted out to the hero of his poem. The
poem was written at a time of renewed hostility with
England: the enmity was not expressed with any degree of
wit, but Harry was the original coiner of a phrase that has
stuck in Scottish usage ever since:

AN I'LL TELL YE ANITHER THING...

Our auld enemys of Saxony's blud
That unto Scotland never sall do gud.

Scots played a substantial part, on the French side, in the
campaigns and battles of the Hundred Years' War that
gradually forced England out of its French possessions. At
Baugé in 1421 a battle almost wholly between English and
Scots was fought. It was not a major engagement but was
well-remembered as a Scottish victory; the historian George
Buchanan noted that the English 'took it in great disdain
that they should be attacked by such an implacable enemy,
not only at home but beyond the seas'. Henry V's death on
campaign occurred after he had ordered the desecration of a
shrine dedicated to St Fiacre, legendary son of a Scottish
king (Gaelic Fiachra). Many believed the saint's curse
struck him with leprosy – and he is said to have died cursing
the Scots and saying 'I can go nowhere without finding
Scotsmen, dead or alive, at my beard.'

*

Before the battle of Flodden in 1513, an anonymous Gaelic
poet wrote verses of encouragement to the earl of Argyll
and his men:

Against Saxons, I say to you,
Lest they rule our country too,
Fight roughly: like the Irish Gael
We will have no English pale.

The English point of view was expressed in *Against the Scots*,
a diatribe by John Skelton, who flourished in the late 15th and
early 16th centuries. Written after the Scottish defeat at
Flodden, it mocks at the pride of the Scots, who appear to
have shown unwillingness to admit that they were beaten:

Against the proud Scots clattering,
That never will leave their tratling: [prattling]

Won they the field, and lost their king?
They may well say, fie on that winning!
Lo, these fond sots
And tratling Scots,
How they are blind
In their own mind,
And will not know   [acknowledge]
Their overthrow
At Branxton Moor!
They are so stour,
So frantic mad,
They say they had
And won the field
With spear and shield.
That is as true
As black is blue
And green is grey.
Whatever they say
Jemmy is dead   [James IV]
And closed in lead,
That was their own king:
Fie on that winning!

*

Skelton was able to have another go in 1532, when the duke
of Albany made an ineffectual invasion of England with a
force of Scottish and French troops. His poem is sarcastically
entitled: *How the Doughty Duke of Albany, like a coward*

knight, ran away shamefully with an hundred tratling Scots and faint-hearted Frenchmen, beside the Water of Tweed.

This duke so fell
Of Albany,
So cowardly,
With all his host
Of the Scottish coast,
For all their boast,
Fled like a beast;
Wherefore to jest
Is my delight
Of this coward knight . . .
Etc., etc.

*

In February 1545, Henry VIII granted a vast extent of the Scottish borderland to Sir Ralph Evers, warden on the English side – if he could conquer it. The Scottish lieutenant of the borders was the earl of Angus, who remarked: 'If they come to take sasine [right of possession] in my lands, I will write the deeds on their backs with sharp pens and bloody ink.' At the battle of Ancrum Moor, Evers' army was scattered by the Scots. Henry VIII made fulminations against Angus, who was unrepentant: 'Little knows King Henry the skirts of Cairntable. I can keep myself there against all his English host.' (But it was not there but at Pinkie on 'Black Saturday' in September 1547 that his army was routed by the earl of Somerset's).

*

At the height of the Spanish Armada crisis in 1588, an advisor of the English state secretary, Walsingham, wrote to warn him that 'England will find Scotland, old Scotland still, and traiterous in the greatest need'.

*

During the 'Bishops' War' of 1638–40, the English poet Sir
William Davenant wrote:

> We feared not the Scots from the High-land nor Low-land;
> Though some of their leaders did craftily brave us,
> With boasting long service in Russe and Poland,
> And with their fierce breeding under Gustavus.

> Not the Tales of their Combats, more strange than
>   Romances,
> Nor Sandy's screw'd Cannon did strike us with wonder;
> Nor their Kettle-drums sounding before their long
>   Launces,
> But Scottish-Court-Whispers struck surer than Thunder.

– it was the court intrigues of Scottish nobles that were
really to be feared. A whiff of treachery is in the air: the
words 'rebel Scot' always came readily to an English
patriotic pen:

> If ever England had occasion
> Her ancient honour to defend,
> Then let her now make preparation,
> Unto an honourable end:
> The factious Scot

Is very hot,
His ancient spleene is ne'er forgot
He long hath bin about this plot.

Our graytious Soveraigne very mildely
Did grant them what they did desire,
Yet they ingratefully and vildly
Have still continued the fire
Of discontent
Gainst government,
But England now is fully bent,
Proud Jocky's bosting to prevent.

– so ran part of *A True Subject's Wish*, from an anonymous supporter of King Charles I.

*

Just about the only time that the Scots created real fear in the English nation – apart from the short panic of late 1745 – was in the first half of the 1640s, when the Scottish army, invading England, was the strongest military force in the country until Cromwell's 'Ironsides' appeared. At first the Scots were allies of the English Parliament, but misunderstandings soon clouded matters, and a war of pamphlets carried accusations and counter-accusations backwards and forwards. A typical title was the Englishman John Lilburne's *An Unhappy Game at Scotch and English, Wherein their Scotch Mists and their Fogs; their sayings and gainsaying; their Juglings, their windings and turnings hither and thither, backwards and forwards, and forwards, backward again . . . detected, discovered and presented to the View of the World as a dreadful Omen and Warning to the Kingdom of England.*

Lilburne protested, in the kind of language more often used by Scots to the English, that 'we will maintain our just Rights and Freedomes in despite of Scots King, or Keysar, though wee welter for it in our blood; and bee it knowne unto you, o yee Men of Scotland, that the free-men of England scorne to bee your Slaves, and they have yet a reserve of gallant blood in their veines, which they will freely spend for their Freedom'.

NEWER WARS

Since 1746, Scottish and English soldiers have fought within the British Army, against other enemies than one another. Despite this, later Scottish ballads returned to the theme of Scottish – English warfare, as in Scott's *All the Blue Bonnets are Bound for the Border*:

Stand to your arms then and march in good order;
England shall many a day
Tell of the bloody fray
When the Blue Bonnets came over the Border.

Or again, in *Wi' a Hundred Pipers*:

Dumbfounder'd the English saw, they saw,
Dumbfounder'd the English ran awa'. . .

English poets did not reciprocate. Their martial bards (oddly enough, usually Scotsmen) were more likely to sing of England's deeds on land and sea against the French.

*

In 1917, during the First World War, the Anglo-Scottish author Ian Hay made a playful comment in a book written for Americans and entitled *The Oppressed English*: 'Today a Scot is leading the British Army in France, another is commanding the British Grand Fleet at sea, while a third directs the Imperial General Staff at home. The Lord Chancellor is a Scot; so are the Chancellor of the Exchequer and the Foreign Secretary. . . Yet no one has ever brought in a bill to give home rule to England!'

The usual British army system put Scots in Scottish regiments and English in English regiments. But increasingly there were units not linked to any country or region, like the Royal Army Ordnance Corps. In the Second World War, the nationalist-minded author George Campbell Hay wrote to Douglas Young of his experiences in the RAOC: 'The Caledonians and South Britons mix no better than oil and water. If you ask about anyone and what sort of person he is the first classification is always "He's wan o' they bloody Englishmen" or "He's a Scotch bastard" and that's the natural attitude you get . . . The most notable characteristic about the English is how docile they are . . . But most of my compatriots, God be thankit, haven't the faintest trace of the spirit of subordination . . . One Aberdonian (we have plenty) eyed a nagging sort of sergeant significantly and said "Did anyone ever hit ye afore, sergeant?" '

A QUESTION OF IDENTITY

In the eighteenth and nineteenth centuries, many Scots were content to describe themselves as English. Scotland's greatest philosopher, David Hume, was one of these, for a time at least. Later he had other thoughts, and wrote to his friend Gilbert Elliot:

I do not believe there is one Englishman in fifty, who, if he heard that I had broke my Neck to night, woud not be rejoic'd with it. Some hate me because I am not a Tory, some because I am not a Whig, some because I am not a Christian, and all because I am a Scotsman. Can you seriously talk of my continuing an Englishman? Am I, or are you, an Englishman? Will they allow us to be so? Do they not treat with Derision our Pretension to that Name, and with Hatred our just Pretension to surpass & govern them? I am a citizen of the World, but if I were to adopt any country, it woud be that in which I live at present . . . (That country was France).

Hume's rhetorical questions are interesting – there is a hint of petulance, of being excluded from a club that is more fun than your own; and of bravado in the pretension to govern the English. At the time Hume wrote, 1764, a Scotsman, Lord Bute, was the king's chief adviser and had been prime minister until the previous year. It was still a novelty to have a Scot in a leading position in the British state: but this was the moment when the jokes about Scots ruling the English began.

Some people tried to promote the term 'British', to the outrage of such populist English politicians as John Wilkes (1725–97), who saw it as a 'melting-down' of Englishness, and whose whipping-up of anti-Scottish prejudice was furiously denounced in Scotland. One Scot, admittedly a lunatic, tried to assassinate him.

RELIGION

One of the ways in which Scots and English got most up each other's noses in the seventeenth century was in their different forms of worship. The Scots went to war when

King Charles I tried to change the constitution of their presbyterian Church. The English were not impressed by Scottish efforts to force them to adopt the same system:

> The *Scots* themselves, that discontented Brood
> Who always loudest for *Religion* bawl,
> (*As those still do wh'have none at all*),
> Who claim so many Titles to be *Jews*,
> (But, surely, such whom God would never for *his People* chuse).

Jonathan Swift (1667–1745), Ode to the King

*

The contradictions that arise between religious belief, greed, and the urge to make money have long been a source of humour:

It is possible to attend all the places of worship of all the denominations from Berwick to the Lizard without gathering any very clear idea as to Who or What the Englishman thinks he is worshipping.

James Bridie, A Small Stir

*

A little Scottish building firm had gained a big contract, but there was a penalty clause on lateness. Work was falling behind and in order to get back on schedule, the owner paid his men extra to work on Sunday. As the workers got busy, he suddenly had a twinge of conscience:

'Don't hammer,' he called to them. 'Use screws.'

*

Sydney Smith claimed that he had studied the subject of the 'Scotch Church' in vain: 'I have not the smallest conception what it is about. I know it has something to do with oatmeal, but beyond that I am in utter darkness.'

*

Edmund Burt noted that a minister in Inverness, in the course of his sermon, urged his congregation to 'fly from the example of a wicked *neighbouring nation*' – the name was unspecified, but nobody thought he meant Ireland.

THE ROUGH SCOT

An English rugby fan met another in their Edinburgh hotel on the morning after England had beaten Scotland and won the Grand Slam at Murrayfield. The friend was sporting a massive black eye.

'Jeremy, old chap, what happened?'

'I was in a pub in the city centre last night, and we were having a perfectly normal discussion about the game, when suddenly this Scotsman leaned over and punched me for no apparent reason.'

*

An Englishman whose childhood holidays in Scotland had given him a romantic fondness for the place decided to retire there. He bought a little house in a Highland glen, and settled in there. There were few neighbours, and none of them paid any attention to him. But he assured himself that it was early days yet. Sure enough, after about a year, one of the neighbours, a massive, bearded figure known as Big Calum, came and knocked on his door.

'You're invited to a party,' said Big Calum. 'Saturday night, my place.'

'Oh, thanks very much,' said the Englishman. 'I'll be delighted to come.'

'It may be a bit noisy,' said Big Calum. 'You know, with a bit of drinking and that, and loud music.'

'That's no trouble,' said the Englishman.

'And it may get a wee bit wild later on. Dancing and stuff.'

'Excellent,' said the Englishman.

'Some folks get a bit carried away, sometimes,' said Big Calum. 'There could be fighting, undressing, sex – anything can happen at a party up here.'

'Er, fine,' said the Englishman. I'm really getting into the people's lives at last, he thought. 'Is it quite formal? What should I wear?'

'Don't worry about that. Come as you are. It'll only be only the two of us,' said Big Calum.

A WOULD-BE SCOURGE OF SCOTLAND –
THE UNSPEAKABLE SCOT

In *The Rise and Fall of the Man of Letters* (1969), John Gross makes a passing reference to 'Lord Alfred Douglas and his obnoxious henchman, T.W.H. Crosland.' Douglas – Oscar Wilde's 'Bosie' – was an Anglo-Scot. Crosland, a literary hack with pretensions to poetry, was the author of a book which once enjoyed some notoriety, *The Unspeakable Scot*, published in 1902. The publisher intended it as the first of a series which would satirise or lampoon various nationalities, but this and Crosland's *Taffy* were the only ones to appear. 'This book is for Englishmen,' it announces. Sadly, it is a rather boring book, with little in it to arouse Scottish fire. His targets are mostly forgotten figures and long-outdated literary cliques and styles, and the techniques and phraseology of anti-semitism, which he held to more sincerely than anti-Scotism, frequently show through: 'Your proper child of Caledonia believes in his rickety bones that he is the salt of the earth. Prompted by a glozing pride, not to say by a black and consuming avarice, he has proclaimed his saltiness from the housetops in and out of season, unblushingly, assiduously, and with results which have no doubt been most satisfactory from his own point of view.' It is a poor last gasp of the robust tradition maintained by Charles Churchill in the eighteenth century. The endpaper of *The Unspeakable Scot* promises *The Egregious Englishman*, by one Angus MacNiell, but it never appeared.

SEX

Among other peoples, neither the English nor the Scots are exactly renowned as sexual performers, whilst as lovers their rating is probably somewhere below the Eskimos. In any situation of national rivalry, however, virility will rise up as a contested area. The Scot, at least when attired in a swash-buckling kilt, probably has the advantage. An explanation is offered by the historian Linda Colley: 'The belief that Scottish Highlanders were unusually well endowed sexually was an old one in the Lowlands and England, reflecting the fact that – like blacks in the American south – they were seen as both threatening and primitive.' (*Britons*)

*

In his satirical poem *The Prophecy of Famine*, Charles Churchill wrote of the Scots: 'Into our places, states and beds they creep' – a reference to Lord Bute's supposed affair with George III's mother. In her study of the forging of the British nation, *Britons*, Linda Colley notes that in the 1760s, 'English insecurity in the face of this new Scottish leverage helps to explain the obsession in so much written and visual polemic at this time with Scottish sexual potency . . . as the princess was made to say in one splendidly filthy cartoon, her hand located firmly under Lord Bute's kilt: "A man of great parts is sure greatly to rise." '

*

. . . the average Englishman dislikes women. He dislikes them even more than the Lowland Scot dislikes them: and that's saying a good deal. . . It is the English who have invented all the ingenious devices for escaping from women's company.

Moray McLaren

*

A Scottish soldier and an English soldier were walking in uniform along a canal bank, chatting together. They came to place where a lusciously pretty girl was sitting, fishing.

'What are you fishing for?' asked the Jock.

'For men,' she replied, archly.

'How come you're sitting on your bait?' said the Jock.

The two soldiers walked on. For about half an hour the Englishman said nothing. Then finally he turned to his friend:

'Jock, that was an awfully funny thing you said to that girl. But how did you know she had worms?'

*

Two smart young French secretaries were strolling along the Champs-Elysées in Paris, when they saw a Scotsman wearing a kilt.

'Look,' said one to the other, 'I've always wondered if they really wear nothing underneath.'

'Let's find out,' said her friend. 'I'll drop a 5-franc piece in front of him, and you get behind him. He's bound to bend over and pick it up, then you'll get a view.'

They followed the plan, and it all happened accordingly. As the Scotsman walked on, tucking the coin into his sporran, the two girls turned to each other.

'Well?' said the one who dropped the coin. 'What's the answer?'

'Ah, you have to look for yourself,' was the reply. 'Let's catch him up. But put down a 50-franc note this time.'

'Why?'

'Because it's worth every cent of it,' replied her friend.

SPEECH

England has many dialects and regional accents, and the form of English that the Scots knew best must for long have been the Geordie tongue of Northumberland which shares many characteristics with Scots. But only two English accents are really acknowledged, the 'lah-di-dah' drawl of the upper classes, associated with the public school system and Oxford; and the h-less speech of the Cockney. Posh English is not so common now as it was when Moray McLaren, in 1949, said that someone talking this way 'really sometimes sounds like a music-hall turn'. He observed that 'Neither in Scotland nor in Ireland do we have this esoteric form of speech. So our people are not accustomed to other people speaking in a special sort of way because they write and think (sic) in a special way.'

*

The Scots have rarely been in doubt as to the quality of their own diction. Speaking of pleading at the bar, Sir George Mackenzie (1636–91) wrote: 'To me it appears undeniable that the *Scotish* idiom of the *British* tongue is more fit for Pleading than either the *English* idiom or the *French* tongue; for certainly a Pleader must use a brisk, smart and quick way of speaking; whereas the *English*, who are a grave nation, use a too slow and grave pronunciation . . . Our Pronunciation is like ourselves, fiery, abrupt, sprightly and bold . . . our Accent is natural, and has nothing, or at least little in it that is peculiar. I say this not to asperse the *English*, they are a Nation I honour, but to reprove the petulancy and malice of some amongst them, who think they do their Country good service, when they reproach ours.

*

Let bragart England in disdain
Ha'd ilka lingo, but her ain:
Her ain, we wat, say what she can,
Is like her true-born Englishman,
A vile promiscuous mungrel seed
O' Danish, Dutch an' Norman breed,
An' prostituted since, to a'
The jargons on this earthly ba'!

Alexander Geddes (1737–1802), Epistle to the Society of Antiquaries

*

At his first meal in Edinburgh, the early eighteenth-century traveller Edmund Burt claimed that the cook offered him the choice of: 'a *duke*, a *fool*, or a *mere-fool*. This was nearly according to his pronunciation; but he meant a duck, a fowl, or a moor-fowl, or grouse.'

*

Henry Mackenzie remembered an anecdote about Lord Elibank, 'a great Scotsman when in England, and a great Englishman when in Scotland'. A neighbour of his in East Lothian was holding forth on the superior qualities of the Scots.

'I don't dispute that,' said Elibank, 'but I think they [the English] do one thing better.'

'You mean, my lord, they make better cheese, but I deny that.'

'No, laird, I only think they speak better English.'

*

The eminent Scottish lawyer John Clerk of Eldin had to go to London to plead before the House of Lords in a property dispute. Clerk spoke with a Scottish accent and at one point he used the word 'enow', the Scots form of 'enough'. The Lord Chancellor, Lord Eldon, stopped him, saying, 'In England, Mr Clerk, we sound the -ough as -uff – *enough*, not *enow*.'

'Verra weel, my Lord,' said Clerk. 'We have said enough of that. I come now to the subdivision of the land in dispute. It was apportioned, my Lord, into what in England you will call *pluff*-land, a pluff-land being as much land as a *pluff*-

man will *pluff* in one day.' The Lord Chancellor interrupted him again, with a laugh this time. 'I think I know *enow* of Scots to follow your argument, Mr Clerk. Pray carry on.' No more corrections were made.

*

A contributor to *Blackwood's Magazine* in 1817 recorded a discussion in an Edinburgh bookshop, when he and a friend, an author, were looking at an old Scots ballad.

'Let me entreat you, for God's sake, to make the language of this ballad so as that we can understand it,' he said to his friend.

'I carena whether ye understand it or no, min; I dinna aye understand it very weel mysel.'

'It is not for what you or I, or any Scotsman, may understand; but remember this must be a sealed book to the English.'

'O, it's a' the better for that – thae English folk like aye best what they dinna understand.'

*

A nineteenth-century *Punch* cartoon showed a Cockney tourist in a Scottish inn.

Cockney Tourist: I'll 'ave a bottle of ale.

Scottish Waitress: Will that be castor ile or paraffin ile, sir?

*

In the 1950s there were many complaints about the ultra-English accents of BBC radio announcers in Scotland. The poet and folklorist Hamish Henderson wrote in a letter to *The Scotsman*: 'If an announcer pronounces 'Boer War' with the accent of Barra or the accent of Buchan, fair enough, but if he pronounces 'Boer War' as if he were a Pekingese barking defiance (*Baw waw! Baw waw*!) he should be out on his neck.

*

On a draughty London Transport escalator, a pretty girl was having trouble preventing her skirt from blowing up.

'A bit airy, isn't it?' said a sympathetic visitor from Scotland, a few steps below.

'What did you expect?' said the girl. 'Feathers?'

SPORT

In sports, Scots and English meet upon equal terms. There is no assumption that one side is specially good or specially bad. Much of each nation's most critical sporting humour is related to the shortcomings of the home side, and not relevant to this book.

An early international was played in 1599 when six Armstrongs from Liddesdale came across the border to Bewcastle to have a game of football with six English lads. Who won is not recorded. After the game they resorted to hard drinking. But there was treachery afoot. An Englishman, William Ridley, had set up an ambush to capture the Armstrongs, all of them wanted men for various raids and crimes in England. But his plan had been leaked, and his ambush was itself attacked by a heavy force. Ridley and two others were killed, thirty prisoners were taken, and 'many sore hurt, especially John Whytfeild whose bowells came out, but are sowed up agane'.

*

The Scottish attitude to English internationals was defined by Bill Shankly on his first game against England, in 1938: '. . . we were Scottish to the core. The wee lion on your dark blue shirt roared out "Get out and kill them." And your heart swelled twice the size.'

*

I thought the greatest moment of my life was this year (1974) on the rain-soaked terraces of Hampden when that second goal went in and we'd beaten the white-shirted swines . . . men, grown men were greetin' like . . . this wee fellow next to me in a big tartan tammy, I threw him in the air. 'We've done it,' I was shouting, 'we've done it,' and there was no way they were going to get two goals back.

And he said, as he was sort of coming down – well I exaggerate a trifle, but I did chuck him up – he said: 'I'm from Shepherd's Bush, mate.' I said, 'Well, what are you wearing that thing for?' And he said, 'It's only for protection, to get into the ground.'

Gordon Williams

In 1961, it had been a different story. The only way the Scots could take any comfort from a 9–3 scoreline was when one fan remarked: 'Mind you, when was the last time we took three goals off England at Wembley?'

*

Although the English cultivate, or used to cultivate, the sense of sportsmanship, James Bridie observed that: 'You will notice that he commends his enemy with a sincere "Well played, Sir," only when he is obviously a beaten enemy.'

*

There is a joke which has been heard in Scotland: 'How

does an Englishman get into the World Cup final? By being the referee.' But this is dangerous ground for Scots. The Scottish attitude at the start of any tournament in which the national side is involved has been described as 'Premature Jock elation'.

*

Jokes about national prowess are less common than jokes about players or supporters:

The day before an International match, the English football side booked in to a big Glasgow hotel. They all came down to dinner together, the coach placing himself at the head of the table. He beckoned to the waiter and said:
    'I'll have a twelve-ounce fillet steak, done medium rare.'
    'And the vegetables, sir?' asked the waiter.
The coach waved an expansive hand.
    'Oh, they'll all have the same.'

*

Scottish (or English fan): What was the score?
English (or Scottish) fan: Nil-nil.
First fan: And at half-time?

*

In 1999 a Yorkshire brewery brought out a special ale called 'Goodbye, Jock' in anticipation of a Scotland–England game.

*

What do you need if you have the supporters of the English football side up to their necks in sand?
A few more tons of sand.

*

Graffito on a pillar of Kingston Bridge, Glasgow: *English Go Home*.
On the next pillar: *Yes, with the Calcutta Cup*.

*

When a leading English rugby player died, he found himself, to his surprise, at the gate of Heaven. St Peter was there, of course.

'We're letting you in here,' he said, 'despite everything, on account of your services to English rugby.'

'Okay,' said the player. 'Just one thing – are there any Scottish players in there?'

'Oh, no, certainly not,' said St Peter.

'That's all right, then,' said the player, and went in, and for the first few days was as happy as any resident of Heaven. But then, going along one day, he heard a roar behind a high wall. Reaching a gate, he went in, and found a rugby game in progress. The star was undoubtedly a tall player with flowing golden hair, golden boots – and wearing what was unmistakably a Scotland strip. The English player watched as the splendid figure scored try after try, converting each one flawlessly. In a rage he left the game and stormed along to see St Peter.

'I thought you said there weren't any Scottish rugby players here,' he said, and described what he had seen.

'Oh,' said St Peter. 'That was just God. He likes to think He's Scottish.'

*

Why do lots of English football teams have Scottish managers, and hardly any Scottish football teams have English managers?
Because good managers can't afford to work in Scotland. And Scottish teams can't afford even bad English managers.

*

A top English Premier League side has a Scottish manager, and one of its top players has a glamorous pop-star wife. One afternoon, the manager announced he had to leave the training session early:

'Carry on, lads,' he said. 'Another two hours of ball-skills practice, then you can go home.'

As soon as he was gone, one of his mates said to the star:

'Why don't we go and have a game of golf instead? The boss will never know.'

'Good idea,' said the star.

So he jumped into his Ferrari and drove home to get his golf clubs. Hearing strange gasping noises from the bedroom, he looked in, and there was the manager vigorously making love to his wife. Quietly he tiptoed away.

On the next training session, the manager again said he had to leave early. His friend once again proposed a game of golf, but this time the ace player shook his head.

'Definitely not,' he said. 'You've no idea how near I got to being caught by the boss last time.'

*

Three small boys playing in a London street were hit by a

garbage truck and killed instantly. Transported to heaven, they were met by St Peter, wringing his hands.

'It's all a dreadful mistake,' he said. 'We got the wrong street. I'm sorry. We're sending you straight back, and to make amends, each of you in twenty years' time will be at the top of his chosen profession. Just state your ambition as you jump off the edge of the cloud.'

The first to jump cried out: 'Lawyer!' Twenty years later he was appointed as a High Court judge.

The second called: 'Doctor!' Twenty years later, he was a highly-paid brain surgeon.

The third, as he stepped off, stumbled and almost tripped. 'Clumsy fool,' he muttered.

Twenty years later, he was named as captain of the England football side.

*

On the other hand, an English football expert was once asked what he thought of Scottish football.

'What a good idea,' he said. 'Why don't they give it a try.'

THE STINGY SCOT

Stinginess was an aspect of Scottish canniness when carried too far – or exaggerated for effect. When the English wanted to mock the Scots, this was the readiest handle to reach for.

What is it that a Scot will not do for money?

William Fowler, sixteenth-century Englishman

*

A man went into a chemist's shop in Aberdeen and left

without picking up his change. The chemist tried to attract his attention by knocking on the window with a sponge.

*

A Scotsman went to the dentist with a raging toothache.

'It will have to come out,' said the dentist.

'What will that cost?' asked the patient.

'Twenty pounds.'

'What will it cost just to loosen it, and I'll pull it out myself?'

*

A Scotsman by mistake put £5 into the church plate as the beadle held it out. He beckoned to the beadle, who bent down, as he whispered:

'Can you treat that as a season?'

*

Englishman: I hear the price of petrol's coming down.
Scotsman: Is that so? What a relief!
Englishman: But you don't own a car.
Scotsman: No, but I have a cigarette-lighter.

*

A Scotsman with a fine mop of hair went past the barber's window. He saw a notice: 'Haircuts £10. Shaves £2.'
He went in, sat down, and said:
  'I want my head shaved.'

*

Out in the Wild West, a Scotsman was among a party attacked by a band of Red Indians. As he ran, pursued by a knife-wielding brave intent on scalping him, he was heard to cry:
  'Don't scalp me, don't scalp me! I paid $5 for a haircut three days ago.'

*

Have you heard about the Scotsman who always counted his money in front of a mirror? It was in case he caught himself cheating.

*

A Scots laird invited some people to dinner at his castle. They sat down at table in a high, cold room, and were served plates with nothing on them but rather unappetising-looking pieces of bread. For a while they gazed at them, then, when the laird began to eat, they rather unenthusiastically followed his example. After a while the laird's servant came in and, approaching his master, whispered:
  'Shall I bring in the hen?'
  'No, no,' said the laird. 'Not yet.'
  He continued to chew on his somewhat stale bread, and the other guests, heartened by the thought of the hen to come, did likewise. Eventually the servant came in again:
  'Is it time for the hen?'
  'I'll call you when it is,' said the laird.
  At last, when the bread was eaten up, the laird called for

his servant, who duly appeared.

'Now bring in the hen,' he said, and the guests sat up expectantly. The servant came in, carrying a live hen in his arms, and set it down on the floor.

'We don't want to waste the crumbs,' said the laird.

TREACHERY

Both Scots and English used to accuse each other of treachery, often for good reason. In times long past, neither side was above breaking its word when it saw an advantage to be gained. In his *History of Greater Britain*, the sixteenth-century Scot John Major notes: 'I have read in histories written by Englishmen that the Scots are the worst of traitors, and that this stain is inborn with them. Not otherwise, if we are to believe these writers, did the Scots overthrow the kingdom and the warlike nation of the Picts. The Scots, on the other hand, call the English the chief of traitors, and, denying that their weapon is a brave man's sword, affirm that all their victories are won by guile and craft.'

Before both countries shared a king, in 1603, this rancour was most felt in the Borders, where Scot faced English, and a whole system of 'Border Law' was in operation to regulate matters. The protocol for arranging a day of truce was designed to avoid tricks. George Macdonald Fraser describes the proceedings: 'On the day itself, the two cavalcades, headed by the respective English and Scottish Wardens, converged on the meeting-place. When they came in view they sat tight and watched each other for a space ... In that brief pause both sides would remember that days of truce had been known to end in open battle; they would pick out the noted troublemakers on each side, and wonder. Then, according to ancient custom, the English Warden would give the word, and one or more of his leading riders would canter across to the Scottish side and ask that assurances of peace be given until the following sunrise . . . The Scottish warden would give the required assurance, and then send riders of his own to ask similar assurance of the English Warden. When this was given, the two Wardens would hold up their hands in token of good faith, and remind their followers to keep the truce. Then and only then would the English Warden and his train advance into Scottish ground, and according to protocol, the Wardens embraced each other. No doubt they sometimes did.'

This, be it noted, was not a meeting in time of war – it was the necessary formula for such a meetings at any time.

*

In 1572, after a failed Catholic rising in the north of England, the earl of Northumberland fled into Scotland for refuge; the Scots handed him back to the English government, for execution. For this, an anonymous English bard reproached them (the text was redone in Scots by a Scottish sympathiser):

Exclamation Made in England

Quho wist to mark the Scottisch gyse,
                              [Who wants, disguise]
Or know the custom of their kyndis
Sall weill persave thair craftie wyse,   [manner]
And fals, dissaitful double myndis:
For quhair as they gud will profes,
The treuth appeiris – they mein no les.

In falset they excel in kynd;   [falsehood]
In wordis thay maist of all exceid;

In treasoun none lyke doe I find;
In treuth thay never observe thair creid;

For, say and promise quhat thay can,
Thair wordes and deidis will never pan.   [match]

A rather feeble effort in self-justification from the Scottish
side came out in response:

Sen France producit ane Ganyelon,
                    [Ganelon: betrayer of Roland]
And England manye traitoris bred,
Quhat fairlie than, thocht we have one?
Yet it is not our Scottish tred . . .

*

False Scot
Sold his king for a groat

– was chanted in England when the Scottish army handed
King Charles I over to the English Parliament. It takes two
to seal a bargain, though.

Thomas Kirke, who wrote *A Modern Account of Scotland* in
1679, was still angry at the Scots' treatment of Charles I

(though it was not the Scots who cut his head off). Writing of the Scottish flag, he says: 'The thistle was wisely placed there, partly to show the fertility of the country; nature alone producing plenty of these gay flowers, and partly as an emblem of the people, the top thereof having some colour of a flower, but the bulk and substance of it, is only sharp and poysonous pricks.'

SOME REFLECTIONS ON THE UNION

Black be the day that e'er to England's ground
Scotland was eikit by the Union's bond.   [linked]

Robert Fergusson (1750–1774)

Scotland has long groaned under the chains of England and knows that its connection there has been the source of its greatest misfortunes. . . We have existed a conquered province these two centuries. We trace our bondage from the Union of the Crown and find it little alleviated by the Union of the Kingdoms . . . the Friends of Liberty in Scotland have almost universally been enemies to Union with England.

Lord Daer (1793)

*

The Scots are a very interesting mob in as much as they made a very interesting deal with the English. A sane deal. It had a lot of problems to it, but the alternative was to have these bastards come up here and kick your arse every twenty-five years.

Alan Sharp

*

The relation the Scots have to the English is a symbiotic one and giving it up is psychologically very difficult because it's going to take away your excuse. With the English there we can say, 'if it wisnae for them bastards . . .'

Alan Sharp

*

Margaret Thatcher, who as prime minister did so much to contribute to the growth of Scottish Nationalism, had this to say in February 1990, in the course of a debate on whether Scotland gained or lost economically by the Union: 'We English, who are a marvellous people, are really very generous to the Scots.'

Her press officer, Sir Bernard Ingham, put his own inimitable gloss on her thoughts, in April of the same year: 'The Scots are subsidised to the damned hilt. The first thing is to stop the Scots grumbling. Emasculate them. That would concentrate their minds. The Scots are getting too much.'

On reading this, one is somehow reminded of a remark by an Irishman, Cyril Connolly, who once described the English as 'sheep with a nasty side'.

*

When the land of the Union Jack boxer shorts makes up its mind, we have no choice but to thole it.

Muriel Gray

WOMEN

In the *Satire Against Scotland*, written in 1617, and generally ascribed to him, Sir Anthony Weldon remarks: 'Thair beastis be generallie small (women excepted), of which sort thair ar no greater in the world.' This is tame beside what he goes on to say: '. . . their flesh naturally abhors cleanliness; their body smells of sweat, and their splay feet never offend in socks. To be chained in marriage with one of them , were to be tied to a dead carcass, and cast into a stinking ditch; formosity and a dainty face are things they dream not of.'

In an *Answer* to this satire, a Scottish writer pretending to be one of Weldon's fellow countrymen says: 'This unclean beast found your wemen too honest for his purpose, and thairfoir voued to plague them thus with his pen.'

An anonymous English writer, a century later, remarked in *Scotland Characterized*: 'Their Women are, if possible, worse than the Men, and carry no Temptations . . . Their Voice is like Thunder . . . It is a very Common Thing for a Woman of Quality to say to her Footman, "Andrew, take a fast Gripe of my Arse, and help me over the Stile." '

*

A Scottish ballad of 1634 records that Scots lasses were impervious to English advances, preferring the 'Blew Cap' of the Scotsman:

> There lived a blithe lass in Faukeland towne,
>> [Falkland]
> And shee had some suitors, I wot not how many;
>> [know]
> But her resolution shee had set downe
> That shee'd have a Blew-Cap gif e'er she had any:
> An Englishman when our good king was there
> Came often unto her, and loved her deere:
> But still she replied, 'Sir, I pray let me be
> Gif ever I have a man, Blew-Cap for me.'

('Our good king' refers to Charles I's coronation visit to Scotland, in 1633.)

*

. . . the difference between the Scotch and the English is that the Scotch are hard in all other respects but soft with women, and the English are soft in all other respects but hard with women.

J. M. Barrie (1860–1937)

*

The traveller Thomas Pennant remarked, of Scottish women: 'The common women are in general most remarkably plain, and soon acquire an old look, and by being much exposed to the weather without hats, such a grin, and contraction of muscles as heightens greatly their natural hardness of features: I never saw so much plainness among the lower rank of females: but the *ne plus ultra* of hard features is not found until you arrive among the fishwives of Aberdeen.'

*

On his return from the House of Lords to the Tower, an old woman, not very well favoured, had pressed through the crowd and screamed in at the window of the coach, 'You'll get that nasty head of yours chopped off, you ugly old Scotch dog,' to which he answered, 'I believe I shall, you ugly old English bitch.'

John Hill Burton, Life of Simon Lord Lovat *(1847), on the trial and execution of Lord Lovat in 1747*

*

Mrs Margaret Stewart Calderwood of Polton made a visit to England in 1756. At the inn at Barnet, north of London, she was met by 'a squinting, smart-like black girl', who spoke to her in what she took to be Irish.

'Are you a Highlander?'
'No,' said she, 'I am Welsh, are you not Welsh?'
'No,' said I, 'but I am Scots, and the Scots and the Welsh are near relations, and much better born than the English.'
'Oh!' said she, 'the maid said you was Welsh, and sent me to see you.'
She took me by the hand, and looked so kindly that I suppose she thought me her relation, because I was not English; which makes me think the English are a people one may perhaps esteem or admire, but they do not draw the affection of strangers, neither in their own country nor out of it.'

AFTERWORD

A survey of the many facets of the Scottish–English relationship can leave the reader feeling as much baffled as edified. So much spleen has been vented, over the centuries, for such a variety of reasons. At the same time, there has been a steady process of convergence in many aspects of life. In the age of instant communication, the differences in social manners and habits between English and Scots have become increasingly cosmetic. This very convergence has prompted separatist urges north of the Border, in order to retain at least some elements of Scottishness. Perhaps, as the more obvious differences are ground down, the Scots find themselves clinging all the more tightly to the mere *fact* of their Scottishness. The English, too, seeing forms of self-government develop to north and west of them, are engaged in a gradual and still somewhat puzzled reappraisal of themselves.

Despite the Scottish obsession with England, the two countries have always existed within a wider European context. This is worth remembering. England's relationship with France was for long not unlike the Scottish–English one. The French, more gifted in elegant laceration than the splenetic Scots, have said sharper things about the English than any Scot has. Perhaps the prize should be awarded to the eighteenth-century Chevalier de Montroux, in conversation with a duchess.

Duchess: Which animal do you think comes nearest to mankind?
Chevalier: The Englishman, duchess.

A good phrase to end with is quoted by Linda Colley in *Britons*. Taken from *The Scotsman* in 1831, it in turn quotes 'a middle class speaker at a mass meeting in Dalkeith', called to celebrate the passing of the Reform Bill in 1831, and referring to both Scots and English: 'We may well consider ourselves as forming members of one great family of freedom.' It is a noble thought from an optimistic moment in British history. Families, of course, do not always share the same ideas, or want to do the same thing at the same time, or even possess mutual respect. Exasperations and indignations are always likely, and fisticuffs not impossible. But when the howling gale comes, or the baying of the wolves is heard outside, then the family knows itself.

Tailpiece – Plus ça change . . .

In September 2002 the *Daily Mail* published an article by Simon Heffer headed: 'Yes, Scots *are* racist, but only to the English'. It described the Scots as a nation 'sunk in corruption, a sense of inadequacy, and above all, a chippy jealousy of its bigger, richer, more outgoing neighbour . . . They can then have a high old time up there, sitting around the peat fires, sipping their whisky and all hating the English together; but however much they do it, it will never make them so happy, wealthy or wise as the folk south of Hadrian's Wall.'

For some reason, the newspaper's Scottish edition did not carry this article.

BIBLIOGRAPHY

Books and Periodicals consulted or quoted from include:

Ascherson, Neal, *Games with Shadows*. London, 1988

Boswell, James, *The Life of Dr Samuel Johnson*. London, 1791

Bridie, James and McLaren, Moray, *A Small Stir: Letters on the English*. London, 1949

Bruce, George, and Scott, Paul H., *A Scottish Postbag*. Edinburgh, 1986

Colley, Linda, *Britons*. London, 1992

Davies, C., *Ethnic Humour*. Bloomington, Ind., 1990

Ferguson, William, *Scotland's Relations with England*. Edinburgh, 1977

Fraser, George Macdonald, *The Steel Bonnets*. London, 1971

Gibbon, Lewis Grassic, and MacDiarmid, Hugh, *Scottish Scene*. London, 1934

Hume Brown, P., *Early Travellers in Scotland*. Edinburgh, 1891

Kamm, Anthony, and Leane, Anne, *A Scottish Childhood*. London, 1985

Kratzmann, G., *Anglo-Scottish Literary Relations*, 1430-1550. Cambridge, 1980

Langford, Paul, *Englishness Identified*. Oxford, 2000

Lindsay, Maurice, *The Discovery of Scotland*. London, 1964

MacDiarmid, Hugh, *Lucky Poet*. London, 1943

Maidment, J., *A Book of Scottish Pasquils*. Edinburgh, 1868

Ross, David, *Scotland: History of a Nation*. Edinburgh, 1999

Ross, David (ed.), *Scottish Quotations*. Edinburgh, 2000

Smith, W. Gordon, *This is My Country*. London, 1981

Blackwood's Magazine
Edinburgh Review
Scottish Historical Review